ANCIENT TRUTHS

THE SCIENCE BEHIND INDIAN TRADITIONS

ASHOK PERSHAD

To all my young friends who have ever wondered about
the meaning behind our age-old traditions. This book is
for you—to inspire curiosity, nurture understanding,
and reveal the wisdom hidden in our heritage

Contents

Foreword

In a world propelled by rapid scientific and technological advancements, we often find ourselves questioning the value of traditions and customs that have guided humanity for centuries. Are these age-old practices mere remnants of a bygone era, or do they carry a timeless wisdom waiting to be rediscovered? Ancient Truths: The Science Behind Indian Traditions offers a compelling answer to this question, taking us on a journey that bridges the past and present with profound clarity and insight.

This book is not a defense of superstition, nor is it an attempt to romanticize antiquity. Instead, it is a thoughtful exploration of how many Indian traditions—often dismissed as irrational or outdated—are rooted in observations of the natural world and the principles of health, sustainability, and well-being. The author has masterfully peeled back layers of cultural heritage to reveal the logic and science interwoven with spiritual wisdom. In doing so, they invite us to view these practices not as relics of the past but as tools for holistic living in the modern age.

The essence of this work lies in its ability to reinterpret ancient practices through the lens of contemporary science. From fasting as a means of detoxification to the environmental wisdom behind tree worship, the book highlights how these traditions align with cutting-edge research in health, ecology, and psychology. It reminds us that while modern science has given us a wealth of knowledge, the scientific spirit—of observation, experimentation, and learning—has long been alive in ancient civilizations, including India.

The relevance of this knowledge extends far beyond individual well-being. In an era grappling with environmental crises, rising lifestyle-related illnesses, and the erosion of cultural identities, ancient Indian traditions offer a roadmap for a balanced and sustainable way of life. They emphasize harmony with nature, respect for resources, and a deep connection to the world around us. Rediscovering these practices not only nurtures our bodies and minds but also reconnects us with our roots, fostering a sense of belonging and purpose.

What makes this book truly remarkable is its tone of curiosity and respect. It neither demands blind adherence to traditions nor dismisses them outright. Instead, it urges readers to approach these ancient practices with an open mind, to question, to understand, and to rediscover. It invites us to appreciate the ingenuity of our ancestors while adapting their wisdom to fit the realities of our time.

As you turn the pages of Ancient Truths: The Science Behind Indian Traditions, I encourage you to reflect on your own connection to the customs and rituals that have shaped your life. Let this book be your guide as you explore the depth and meaning behind practices you may have once overlooked or misunderstood. In embracing this journey, you may find not only the answers to age-old mysteries but also the tools to lead a healthier, more harmonious life.

This is not just a book; it is an invitation to rediscover the wisdom of the past and bring it to life in the present. Accept the invitation with curiosity, and you may find yourself inspired by the timeless relevance of these ancient truths.

PREFACE

Tradition and science—two words that often seem to exist at odds with each other. One is seen as rooted in the past, cloaked in rituals and beliefs, while the other is heralded as a beacon of progress, driven by evidence and logic. Yet, a closer look reveals that these two forces are not adversaries but rather companions in humanity's journey of understanding the world. This realization forms the foundation of Ancient Truths: The Science Behind Indian Traditions.

For centuries, Indian traditions have carried an air of mystery, often regarded as superstitions or mere cultural quirks. Many of these practices have been dismissed in the name of modernization, while others have been followed without question or comprehension. However, beneath the surface lies a reservoir of knowledge—practical, scientific, and profoundly relevant to our modern lives. This book was born out of a desire to explore these traditions, to sift through the sands of time and uncover the gems of wisdom that continue to shine in today's context.

The journey of writing this book has been one of discovery and rediscovery. As I delved into practices that shaped my own upbringing, I began to see them in a new light. Customs like lighting lamps, fasting, or planting sacred trees are not just symbolic gestures but are deeply intertwined with health, environmental sustainability, and community well-being. They reflect a harmonious relationship with nature, a keen observation of human biology, and an innate understanding of how to foster balance in life.

At the heart of this book lies a simple yet profound truth: our ancestors were observers, scientists in their own right. Their understanding of the world was shaped not by laboratories but by centuries of lived experience, trial, and refinement. They crafted traditions not out of whimsy but out of a deep respect for the forces of nature and a desire to align human life with them. By exploring these practices with a scientific lens, we can reconnect with this wisdom, not to replicate it blindly but to adapt it thoughtfully to our modern context.

In these pages, you will find explanations for practices you may have grown up with but never fully understood. More importantly, you will discover how these ancient truths can enrich your life today—whether by promoting health, fostering mindfulness, or encouraging sustainable living.

This book is not an exhaustive catalog of Indian traditions, nor does it claim to have all the answers. Instead, it is an invitation to approach our heritage with curiosity and respect. It is a call to bridge the gap between science and tradition, to appreciate the depth of our cultural roots, and to find ways to integrate this wisdom into our fast-paced, modern lives.

As you embark on this journey, I hope this book ignites a spark of inquiry within you. May it encourage you to question, explore, and embrace the richness of traditions with an open mind. Together, let us celebrate the timelessness of Indian wisdom and its enduring relevance in today's world.

With gratitude and hope,
Ashok Pershad

I
Introduction

Why Ancient Wisdom Matters in the Modern World?

In a world dominated by technology and rapid scientific advancements, it's easy to dismiss ancient traditions as outdated or irrelevant. Many practices, particularly those rooted in Indian culture, are often labeled as superstitions or blind faith. Yet, if we pause to explore the origins of these customs, we often find they were founded on keen observations of nature, practical health considerations, or an intuitive understanding of human behavior.

The disconnect between modernity and tradition arises from the lack of context. Our ancestors didn't have the tools to explain their practices in terms of modern science, so they often framed them in ways that were relatable and enforceable within their cultural and social framework. For example, asking someone not to eat food during an eclipse might have sounded more convincing when tied to divine consequences than to the reality of food spoilage due to changing environmental conditions.

This book aims to bridge that gap. It's a journey into understanding the "why" behind Indian traditions—uncovering the wisdom beneath the surface of practices that have stood the test of time.

The Relevance of Ancient Wisdom Today

In today's fast-paced world, we often find ourselves grappling with challenges like environmental degradation, mental health crises, and the loss of community and connection. Ironically, many solutions to these issues can be found in ancient traditions:

- Environmental conservation was ingrained in the practice of worshipping trees and rivers.
- Mindfulness and mental well-being were fostered through rituals, prayers, and meditation.
- Dietary practices emphasized balance and seasonal eating, which modern nutritionists now advocate.
- By revisiting these practices with an open mind, we can rediscover tools for living harmoniously with ourselves and our surroundings.

From Myth to Meaning

A key question we'll address throughout this book is: Are these traditions superstitions, or do they hold deeper truths? To answer this, we'll explore the origins of these practices and examine their scientific, cultural, and environmental underpinnings. In doing so, we'll see that ancient wisdom wasn't arbitrary—it was rooted in observation, experience, and a profound understanding of the world.

Why Now?

The resurgence of interest in holistic living, Ayurveda, yoga, and sustainable practices is a testament to the relevance of ancient wisdom. As global challenges push us to rethink how we live, it's worth revisiting the traditions that prioritized balance, respect for nature, and community welfare.

What to Expect

Each chapter of this book delves into specific customs—explaining the myths, decoding their significance, and revealing the truths hidden within. Whether it's the rationale behind fasting, the symbolism of rituals, or the environmental wisdom of sacred practices, this book will show you that the past holds valuable lessons for the present.

Let's embark on this journey together and discover how the wisdom of the past can illuminate our path forward.

Superstition vs. Science: Understanding the Context

To truly appreciate the wisdom behind ancient practices, we must first understand how they came to be misunderstood as superstitions. Over centuries, the original intent of many customs became obscured, simplified, or even distorted. Without a clear explanation of their purposes, these practices began to be seen as rituals to be followed blindly, rather than as methods grounded in logic or observation.

For instance, consider the belief in hanging a lemon and chilies at doorways to ward off evil spirits. While this may seem like superstition, the practice originated as a natural pest repellent. The acidic juice of lemons and the pungent compounds in chilies deterred insects, helping to maintain hygiene in households. Over time, as scientific reasoning was not widely communicated, this practical measure was explained through spiritual narratives, making it easier for the masses to adopt.

Similarly, the practice of clapping hands during prayers or singing bhajans was not merely a display of devotion. It also served a health purpose—stimulating acupressure points on the palms, which helped improve circulation and energy flow in the body.

Why Science Got Lost in Translation

- Lack of Documentation: Most ancient wisdom was passed down orally, leading to loss or distortion of its original meaning.
- Cultural Simplification: To make practices widely acceptable, explanations were often tied to religion or morality.
- Colonial and Modern Influence: During colonial rule and later, modernity led to the dismissal of traditional practices as backward or irrelevant.
- Evolving Contexts: Some practices made sense in their original settings but lost relevance in changing times, leading to skepticism.

Reconnecting with Logic

Reframing these traditions through the lens of science doesn't diminish their cultural or spiritual significance.

Instead, it enhances our understanding and allows us to honor these customs with newfound respect. For instance, when we understand the environmental logic of worshipping rivers, we're more likely to protect these vital ecosystems. When we learn the health benefits of fasting, it becomes more than just a religious obligation.

II

Household Practices

The customs we observe at home often go unnoticed, blending seamlessly into daily life. These small yet significant practices have been passed down through generations, sometimes without a clear explanation of their origins or purpose. Yet, they hold valuable lessons rooted in science, hygiene, and well-being.

Let's explore some common household traditions and uncover the wisdom behind them.

1. Lemon and Chilies at Doorways

The Practice: In many Indian households, it is a common sight to see a string of green chilies and lemons hanging at the entrance of homes, shops, or temples. This practice is often seen as a protective measure against evil or negative energy, and it is believed to bring good luck and ward off misfortune.

The Truth:

- **Cultural and Spiritual Belief:** The lemon and chilies are considered to have strong protective powers. The combination is believed to protect the home from evil spirits, the "evil eye" (nazar), and negative energies. In traditional Indian culture, it was thought that these hanging items could act as a shield, deflecting bad energy or the ill will of others.

- **Antibacterial Properties:** Lemon and green chilies have natural antibacterial and antiseptic properties. The lemon, rich in citric acid, can kill bacteria and pathogens that may be present in the air. Chilies contain capsaicin, which has antimicrobial effects as well. In a time when traditional remedies were often the only available options for hygiene and sanitation, these properties may have contributed to the belief that the hanging of these items would purify the environment around the home.

- **Insect Repellent:** The pungent smell of chilies is known to repel insects, especially mosquitoes and flies. This would have been particularly useful in earlier times when homes lacked modern pest control solutions. The combination of the sharp, tangy lemon scent and the strong odor of chilies might have kept unwanted insects at bay, thus making the home environment cleaner and healthier.

- **Aromatherapy and Healing**: Both lemon and chilies are known to have positive effects on mood and health. Lemon is often used in aromatherapy to refresh and uplift the mind, providing clarity and reducing stress. Chilies, on the other hand, have a warming effect on the body, improving circulation and potentially stimulating the senses. This sensory stimulation could contribute to a more positive and energized atmosphere in the home.
- **A Symbol of Purification**: The use of lemon and chilies at the entrance also symbolizes purification. Just as one washes their hands or takes a bath to cleanse themselves physically, the practice of hanging these items is seen as a way of purifying the space, symbolically "cleaning" the threshold of the home. It creates a mental and spiritual boundary that separates the sacred and the mundane.

2. Drawing Rangoli

The Practice: Rangoli is a traditional Indian art form that involves creating intricate, colorful patterns on the floor, typically at the entrance of homes, during festivals, or on special occasions. The designs are made using materials such as colored powders, rice flour, flower petals, and even colored sand. This practice is especially popular during Diwali, but it is also seen during other festivals and celebrations.

The Truth:

- **Feng Shui and Vastu Influence**: Rangoli is often created in areas that are considered important in the principles of Vastu Shastra (the Indian equivalent of Feng Shui), such as the entrance or central courtyard. According to

Vastu, the correct placement of Rangoli enhances the flow of positive energy (prana) and helps dispel negative energies. The design and colors used in Rangoli also correspond to different elements, enhancing the balance of those elements within the home.

- **Psychological Impact:** The act of drawing Rangoli itself is calming and meditative. Engaging in the creative process helps to reduce stress, promote mindfulness, and foster a sense of accomplishment. The colors and patterns can uplift the spirits, bringing joy and a sense of peace to those who engage in the activity.
- **Air Purification and Antimicrobial Benefits:** Traditionally, Rangoli was made with rice flour, which has been shown to attract ants and small insects. This was not only a way to keep pests away but also a natural way to reduce the number of such insects inside the home. Additionally, many of the materials used in Rangoli, like turmeric, have antimicrobial properties, contributing to the cleanliness and purification of the space.
- **Use of Natural Elements:** In earlier times, Rangoli was created using natural materials like turmeric, rice flour, and flower petals, which were not only biodegradable but also served ecological purposes. Flower petals, for example, would decompose and contribute to the soil's health. The colors used in Rangoli were derived from natural sources, further aligning with the practice of using sustainable, environment-friendly materials.
- **Aesthetic Tradition:** Rangoli is seen as a form of art that beautifies the home, making it more welcoming for guests and deities. In Hindu culture, drawing Rangoli at the entrance symbolizes the welcoming of good energy, positivity, and prosperity. The designs are believed to

invite Lakshmi, the Goddess of Wealth, into the home during festivals, particularly Diwali.

- **Geometrical Patterns:** The patterns in Rangoli often follow symmetrical or geometrical designs that represent cosmic harmony, order, and balance. Such symmetry is believed to create an aura of peace and stability within the home, contributing to a positive energy flow and creating an environment conducive to prosperity and well-being.

3. Tulsi Plant Care

The Practice: The Tulsi (Holy Basil) plant is revered in Hindu culture for its spiritual and medicinal properties. It is often grown in homes, especially in courtyards or near the entrance, where it is taken care of with great reverence. The plant is used in daily worship, and its leaves are offered to deities, particularly Lord Vishnu and Lord Krishna. Tulsi is also considered a symbol of purity and is often referred to as "the queen of herbs."

The Truth:

- **Health and Medicinal Benefits:** Tulsi possesses numerous health benefits. It helps reduce stress, balance hormones, and improve digestion. It also supports the respiratory system by clearing congestion and improving lung function.
- **Spiritual Significance:** Tulsi is considered sacred, purifying the home and dispelling negative energy. It is believed to enhance the spiritual energy of a household and protect it from misfortune.

- **A Natural Insect Repellent:** The plant's strong aroma naturally repels mosquitoes and other harmful insects, making it an eco-friendly alternative to chemical repellents.
- **Gardening and Care:** Tulsi requires minimal care, thriving in sunny spots with regular watering. It is an easy-to-grow plant that can be maintained even in small spaces, making it ideal for urban gardens.
- **Connection to Holistic Living:** Caring for Tulsi encourages individuals to adopt a holistic approach to life, integrating environmental care, health practices, and spiritual devotion into their daily routine.

4. Burning Camphor in the Evening

The Practice: Camphor is a chemical that used to be made by distilling the bark and wood of the camphor tree. Burning camphor during evening prayers or rituals is a common practice in many Hindu households. The camphor is typically lit as part of the aarti or prayer ceremony, where it is offered to deities. The burning of camphor produces a pleasant aroma and is often considered an important ritualistic activity for purifying the surroundings.

The Truth:

- **Purification of the Environment:** The act of burning camphor is believed to purify the air by releasing negative ions that neutralize harmful bacteria, viruses, and pollutants in the surrounding environment.
- **Mental Clarity and Calmness:** The aroma released by burning camphor is said to have a calming effect on the mind, reducing stress and promoting mental clarity and

focus. It is often used in meditation practices to enhance concentration.

- **Symbol of Purity:** Camphor, when it burns completely without leaving any residue, symbolizes purity and the burning away of impurities, both in the environment and within oneself. It signifies the removal of negative thoughts and energies.
- **Spiritual Upliftment:** In Hindu rituals, the offering of camphor during prayers is believed to invoke divine blessings, purify the surroundings, and foster a higher state of spiritual consciousness. Its fragrance is considered an offering to the gods.
- **Antibacterial and Antiseptic Properties:** Camphor is known for its antiseptic qualities. Burning it in the evening can help disinfect the air and reduce the presence of harmful microorganisms, thus improving the overall health of the household.
- **Symbolic of Detachment:** Camphor's complete combustion, which leaves no trace behind, is often seen as a metaphor for life and death. It reminds devotees of the transient nature of material life and encourages them to focus on spiritual growth and detachment from worldly possessions.
- **Support for Respiratory Health:** The smoke from burning camphor is believed to help clear the respiratory passages, making it beneficial for people suffering from colds or other respiratory conditions.

5. Sweeping After Sunset

The Practice: In many Hindu households, it is considered inauspicious to sweep the house after sunset. This belief stems from traditional values and practices, often with cultural and spiritual connotations. While this might seem superstitious at first glance, deeper reasoning reveals practical and symbolic insights.

The Truth:

- **Preservation of Valuables:** In ancient times, homes were lit by oil lamps or candles, making it challenging to see clearly at night. Sweeping after sunset could lead to accidentally discarding small, valuable items like coins or jewelry, as they might be mistaken for dirt in dim light. Avoiding this practice was a way to prevent such losses.
- **Symbolism of Wealth and Prosperity:** In Hinduism, Lakshmi, the goddess of wealth, is believed to visit homes in the evening. Sweeping after sunset is thought to disturb her blessings or drive away prosperity. This symbolic reasoning served to emphasize respect for resources and gratitude for abundance.
- **Energy and Vastu Principles:** Some Vastu Shastra principles suggest that sweeping after sunset may disrupt the positive energy flow in the home. While this lacks direct scientific backing, the concept ties to maintaining harmony in living spaces, an essential aspect of mental and emotional well-being.
- **Practical Considerations:** Dust and debris stirred up by sweeping can aggravate allergies or respiratory issues, especially at night when airflow inside homes is typically reduced. Avoiding sweeping in the evening could minimize these health concerns.
- **Modern Context:** With advancements in lighting and cleaning technologies, the original practical reasons for this belief are less relevant today. However, the tradition

remains a gentle reminder of mindful housekeeping and care for one's environment.

6. Breaking Glass or Mirror as a Bad Omen

The Practice: In many cultures, especially in Indian households, breaking a glass or mirror is considered a bad omen, often seen as a sign of impending misfortune or negative energy.
The Truth:

- **Safety Concerns:** Historically, breaking glass or mirrors could have led to injuries or dangerous situations, which is why it was considered an ill omen. The belief may have originated as a cautionary measure to avoid harm from broken glass.
- **Symbolic of Self-Reflection:** Mirrors are often associated with self-reflection and one's inner state. Breaking a mirror was thought to signify a disruption in self-awareness or mental peace, symbolizing an imbalance in personal or spiritual life.
- **Energy Disruption:** In Vastu Shastra (traditional Indian architecture), mirrors are believed to reflect energy. A broken mirror is seen as a disruption of positive energy in the home, leading to confusion and negativity.
- **Psychological Impact:** The belief in mirrors as symbols of one's identity may have led to the superstition. The thought of breaking a mirror could evoke anxiety or worry, which in itself could create a negative atmosphere.

Conclusion

Household practices often reflect the wisdom of a time when people lived in closer harmony with their environment. While the world has changed, many of these traditions still hold relevance, offering practical benefits and fostering a sense of mindfulness and community.

III

Health and Hygiene

Health and hygiene have always been fundamental aspects of Indian culture. Long before modern medicine, our ancestors developed practices to maintain physical well-being and prevent diseases. These habits were deeply integrated into daily life, often under the guise of rituals or customs.

By examining these traditions through a scientific lens, we can see how they contribute to personal and community health.

1. Daily Bathing Rituals

The Practice: Taking a daily bath, especially in the morning, is a common ritual in many Indian households. It is often done before prayers or starting daily activities.

The Truth:

- **Hygiene and Health:** Bathing daily helps remove sweat, dirt, and toxins from the body, preventing skin infections and promoting overall hygiene. The practice aligns with modern health recommendations for maintaining cleanliness and well-being.
- **Symbol of Purity:** In many traditions, a bath before prayers is considered a way to purify oneself physically and mentally, preparing for a spiritual or meditative practice.
- **Stimulates Blood Circulation:** The act of bathing, especially with warm water, improves blood circulation, helping to energize the body for the day ahead.
- **Mental Clarity and Focus:** Bathing has a calming effect on the mind. The ritual of washing away the day's stress fosters mental clarity and refreshes the mind for the tasks ahead.
- **Temperature Regulation:** Bathing with cool water in the morning or evening helps maintain body temperature, especially in hot climates, ensuring comfort and well-being.
- **Cultural and Social Bonding:** Bathing rituals, such as in a river or with family, strengthen social bonds and maintain cultural continuity. In many communities, the practice also reinforces discipline and a sense of routine.

2. Washing Hands and Feet Before Entering the Home

The Practice: It is a common practice in many Indian households to wash hands and feet before entering the house, particularly after coming back from outside or before meals.

The Truth:

- **Hygiene and Cleanliness:** Washing hands and feet removes dirt, dust, and bacteria collected from outdoor environments, helping maintain a clean and hygienic living space. This is a basic health practice, in line with modern hygiene standards.
- **Symbolic Purification:** The act of washing hands and feet is seen as a symbolic purification of the body, helping to rid oneself of external impurities before entering a sacred or personal space. It prepares the body for rituals, prayers, or shared meals, creating a sense of mental and physical readiness.
- **Preventing Contamination:** The feet, especially, are in direct contact with the ground, which can carry harmful microbes. Washing them ensures that harmful pathogens are not carried inside, reducing the risk of spreading infections in the home.
- **Cultural Practice for Respect:** In many cultures, washing hands and feet before entering the home also represents respect for the space and the people in it. It is an acknowledgment of cleanliness and discipline, reinforcing the value of maintaining a pure environment.
- **Mental Reset:** This simple act has a calming and grounding effect, helping individuals mentally

transition from the outside world to a space of rest and peace, creating a boundary between external distractions and home life.

3. Eating with Hands

The Practice: In many Indian households, eating with hands is a common practice, particularly during meals like lunch and dinner.
The Truth:

- **Enhanced Digestion:** Eating with hands engages the brain's sensory neurons, preparing the digestive system for food. The act of touching food triggers the release of digestive enzymes, aiding in better digestion and absorption of nutrients.
- **Connection with Food:** Eating with hands creates a tactile connection to the food, heightening the awareness of textures, temperatures, and flavors, which fosters mindfulness during meals. This practice encourages gratitude for the food and a deeper appreciation for the sensory experience.
- **Improved Portion Control:** Eating with hands helps in controlling portions more intuitively. The act of using fingers to scoop food naturally limits overeating, as it requires more attention to the food being consumed.
- **Stimulating Taste Buds:** The fingertips are sensitive to temperature and texture, which enhances the overall taste experience. Eating with hands allows for better tactile feedback, helping people enjoy the full range of flavors in their food.

- **Aligning with Nature:** The practice of eating with hands connects individuals to the natural world, reminding them of the earth's bounty and creating a mindful eating experience that aligns with holistic living.

4. Oil Pulling

The Practice: Oil pulling involves swishing a tablespoon of oil (usually coconut, sesame, or sunflower oil) in the mouth for about 15-20 minutes before spitting it out. This practice is often done in the morning on an empty stomach.

The Truth:

- **Oral Health Benefits:** Oil pulling is an ancient practice mentioned in Ayurvedic texts, known for its ability to remove toxins (called "ama") from the mouth. It helps reduce plaque, prevent cavities, and maintain overall oral hygiene by targeting harmful bacteria and microbes.
- **Improves Gum Health:** Regular oil pulling can help reduce gingivitis, inflammation, and gum disease by strengthening the gums and preventing the buildup of harmful bacteria that contribute to oral infections.
- **Detoxification:** According to Ayurveda, oil pulling is thought to pull out toxins from the body through the mouth. While this is still under scientific review, oil pulling can stimulate the salivary glands, which may help in cleansing and detoxifying the oral cavity.
- **Reduces Bad Breath:** By eliminating bacteria that cause bad breath (halitosis), oil pulling can promote fresher breath throughout the day.

- **Strengthens Jaw and Teeth:** The mechanical action of swishing oil helps in toning the jaw muscles, which can aid in reducing tooth sensitivity and even help maintain overall tooth strength.

5. Using Neem Twigs for Oral Hygiene

The Practice: In many Indian households, neem twigs (also known as "datun") have been used for centuries as a natural toothbrush. People chew on one end of the neem twig until it becomes frayed, and then use it to brush their teeth.
The Truth:

- **Antibacterial Properties:** Neem contains natural antibacterial, antiviral, and antifungal properties. The compounds in neem help reduce the growth of harmful bacteria in the mouth, promoting oral health and preventing gum disease, tooth decay, and bad breath.
- **Gum Health:** Chewing on neem twigs helps massage the gums, increasing blood circulation, and strengthening gum tissue. The antibacterial properties also protect against gingivitis, reducing inflammation and promoting overall gum health.
- **Natural Teeth Whitening:** Neem has mild abrasives that help in the gentle removal of plaque and stains from teeth, naturally whitening them over time without the use of harsh chemicals.
- **Prevents Cavities and Tooth Decay:** The antimicrobial properties of neem help protect the teeth from cavities by inhibiting the growth of harmful bacteria that contribute to tooth decay. Regular use of neem twigs has been shown to be effective in reducing plaque

formation.

- **No Toxic Chemicals**: Unlike many modern toothpaste brands, neem twigs are free from chemicals like fluoride and artificial additives. This makes them a natural, eco-friendly alternative for oral hygiene.

6. Turmeric for Wounds

The Practice: Applying turmeric powder or a paste made from turmeric and water to cuts, scrapes, or bruises is a common remedy in many Indian households.

The Truth:

- **Antiseptic and Antibacterial Properties**: Turmeric contains curcumin, a compound with powerful antiseptic and antibacterial qualities. When applied to wounds, it helps prevent infection by inhibiting the growth of bacteria and other pathogens.
- **Accelerates Healing**: Curcumin has anti-inflammatory properties that can help reduce swelling and pain in wounds. It also stimulates tissue regeneration, promoting faster healing and reducing scarring.
- **Reduces Pain and Inflammation**: Turmeric is known for its ability to reduce pain and inflammation. By applying turmeric paste to a wound, it can alleviate discomfort and calm the surrounding tissues, helping the body heal more efficiently.
- **Natural Antioxidant**: Turmeric is a potent antioxidant, which helps to neutralize free radicals in the body and protect cells from oxidative damage. This antioxidant effect can aid in faster and more effective recovery from wounds.

- **Promotes Skin Health:** Besides healing wounds, turmeric also nourishes the skin and improves its overall health. It can help prevent skin discoloration or scarring from minor injuries, keeping the skin clear and even-toned.

7. Fasting for Health

The Practice: Fasting, a common tradition in many cultures and religions, including Hinduism, involves abstaining from food or drink for a specific period. In India, fasting is often observed on certain days like Ekadashi or during festivals as a form of purification or spiritual practice.
The Truth:

- **Detoxification:** Fasting allows the body to rest and detoxify. When not engaged in digestion, the body can focus on cleansing itself, flushing out toxins, and repairing cells. This process supports the liver and kidneys in removing waste from the body, promoting overall wellness.
- **Improves Metabolism:** Periodic fasting can enhance metabolic function. When you fast, the body switches from using glucose for energy to using stored fat, which helps in reducing fat and improving metabolic health. This process, known as ketosis, is beneficial for weight management and energy balance.
- **Supports Cellular Repair:** Fasting triggers a process called autophagy, where the body breaks down and removes dysfunctional cells. This repair mechanism has been linked to improved cell regeneration, immune function, and a reduction in the risk of chronic diseases.

- **Improves Insulin Sensitivity:** Fasting has been shown to increase insulin sensitivity, reducing the risk of type 2 diabetes. By lowering blood sugar levels and allowing insulin to function more effectively, fasting supports healthy blood sugar regulation.
- **Spiritual and Mental Clarity:** Beyond physical benefits, fasting is seen as a way to clear the mind and foster spiritual growth. The discipline involved in fasting sharpens focus and promotes mental clarity, providing an opportunity for self-reflection and mindfulness.
- **Boosts Longevity:** Scientific studies have shown that intermittent fasting may contribute to increased lifespan by reducing the risk of age-related diseases and promoting healthier aging. The cellular benefits of fasting help in slowing down the aging process and enhancing longevity.

8. Keeping Shoes Outside the House

The Practice: It is common in many households, particularly in India, to leave shoes outside the door or on a designated mat before entering the house. This practice is deeply rooted in both cultural and practical traditions.

The Truth:

- **Preventing Dirt and Germs:** Shoes carry dirt, bacteria, and germs from the outside environment. Keeping them outside helps prevent these harmful substances from being brought into the home, maintaining cleanliness and reducing the risk of infections.
- **Symbol of Respect:** In many cultures, particularly in India, shoes are considered unclean because they come

into contact with the ground. By leaving them outside, people show respect for the purity of the home, which is considered a sacred space. This practice also aligns with the cultural belief of maintaining spiritual and physical cleanliness.

- **Air Quality and Hygiene:** Shoes, especially those worn outdoors, can carry dust, allergens, and even chemicals. By keeping them outside, the air quality inside the home is improved, reducing the chances of respiratory issues or allergic reactions.
- **Energy and Spiritual Significance:** In many traditional beliefs, the act of leaving shoes outside symbolizes the removal of negative energy before entering a sacred space. The house is considered a place of rest, peace, and positivity, and this simple practice helps preserve that harmony by preventing the entry of any disruptive or negative influences.
- **Practical Health Benefits:** The soles of shoes often accumulate bacteria, fungus, and other microorganisms, which can contribute to foot infections and other health concerns. By removing shoes before entering the house, this reduces the risk of spreading these health hazards into living spaces.

9. Turmeric Milk as a Remedy

The Practice: Turmeric milk, also known as "golden milk," is a traditional remedy commonly consumed in many Indian households, especially during cold weather or when someone is feeling unwell. It involves adding turmeric to warm milk, often with a pinch of black pepper, and drinking it as a health tonic.

The Truth:

- **Anti-Inflammatory Properties:** Turmeric contains curcumin, a powerful compound known for its anti-inflammatory effects. When consumed, it can help reduce inflammation in the body, making it an effective remedy for conditions like arthritis, muscle pain, and general aches.
- **Boosts Immunity:** The combination of turmeric and milk enhances the body's immune response. Turmeric's antibacterial and antiviral properties help fight infections, while milk provides essential nutrients like calcium and vitamin D, which support overall immune health.
- **Digestive Health:** Turmeric has been used for centuries to improve digestion. It stimulates bile production, which helps in the digestion of fats. Additionally, it can relieve symptoms of indigestion, bloating, and gas.
- **Improves Sleep Quality:** Drinking warm turmeric milk before bedtime can promote better sleep. The warmth of the milk helps relax the body, while turmeric has been known to have calming effects on the nervous system, making it a natural sleep aid.
- **Antioxidant Rich:** Turmeric milk is rich in antioxidants, which help neutralize harmful free radicals in the body. This can contribute to healthier skin, reduce oxidative stress, and lower the risk of chronic diseases such as cancer.
- **Natural Cold and Cough Remedy:** Turmeric has long been used to treat respiratory issues, such as the common cold and cough. Its antimicrobial properties help fight off infections, while the soothing qualities of milk provide comfort for a sore throat or cough.

10. Using Earthen Pots for Water Storage

The Practice: Storing water in earthen pots, or "matkas," is a common tradition in India, especially in rural areas. These unglazed clay pots are used to store drinking water and are believed to keep it cool and fresh, especially during hot weather.

The Truth:

- **Natural Cooling:** One of the key benefits of earthen pots is their ability to cool water naturally. The porous nature of clay allows water to evaporate from the surface of the pot. As the water evaporates, it absorbs heat from the surrounding water, lowering the temperature and keeping it cool without the need for refrigeration. This process is known as evaporative cooling.
- **Alkaline Water:** Clay pots are naturally alkaline, which can help balance the pH level of the water. Drinking water stored in earthen pots may help reduce acidity in the body, contributing to overall health. The minerals released by the clay can also provide some additional nutrients to the water.
- **Improved Hydration:** Water stored in earthen pots is believed to be more hydrating. The natural properties of the clay can improve the taste and freshness of water, making it more refreshing and encouraging proper hydration.
- **Antimicrobial Properties:** The natural composition of clay has antimicrobial qualities. Research has shown that earthen pots can help reduce the growth of harmful bacteria and microbes in stored water, making it safer to drink compared to water stored in plastic containers.

- **Sustainability:** Unlike plastic containers, which are often harmful to the environment, earthen pots are eco-friendly. They are made from natural, renewable resources and are biodegradable, making them a sustainable choice for water storage.
- **Cultural and Spiritual Significance:** In many Indian households, earthen pots are also seen as a symbol of harmony with nature and tradition. Using clay pots for water storage is a way to honor cultural practices while maintaining a connection to nature and the earth.

11. Applying Kajal (Kohl) to Eyes

The Practice: Kajal, also known as kohl, is a traditional eye cosmetic used by many people, particularly in India, to line the eyes. It is commonly applied to the waterline or around the eyes for aesthetic purposes, and is often considered a symbol of beauty, protection, and tradition.

The Truth:

- **Protects from Eye Infections:** Traditional kajal is often made from natural ingredients like soot from oil lamps, almonds, and other herbs. These ingredients have antibacterial properties, which can help protect the eyes from infections like conjunctivitis or irritation. In ancient times, applying kajal was believed to keep the eyes healthy and free from harmful pathogens.
- **Improves Vision:** In Ayurvedic practices, kajal is thought to strengthen the eyes and improve vision. The ingredients used in making traditional kajal, such as castor oil and ghee, are believed to nourish the delicate skin around the eyes and improve eye health.

- **Reduces Sunlight Sensitivity:** Kajal can help reduce the glare of bright sunlight, especially in regions where intense sunlight is prevalent. By lining the waterline, it helps shield the eyes from excessive light, which may reduce discomfort and strain.
- **Enhances Eye Health:** The practice of applying kajal is often linked to promoting eye health. It is believed that regular use can help in the prevention of conditions like cataracts, eye fatigue, and irritation caused by exposure to dust or pollutants.
- **Cultural and Spiritual Significance:** Kajal is not just a cosmetic product; it carries spiritual significance in many cultures. It is often applied to newborns to protect them from the "evil eye" (negative energies) and bring good fortune. In this context, kajal serves as a form of spiritual protection.
- **Natural Cooling Effect:** The coolness of kajal can be soothing, especially in hot climates. Its cooling effect on the eyes is also thought to reduce symptoms like redness or irritation caused by heat.

12. Using Copper Vessels for Drinking Water

The Practice: Storing and drinking water from copper vessels, such as copper bottles or glasses, is a common tradition in India. It is believed that drinking water from copper vessels can have several health benefits, and this practice has been followed for centuries.

The Truth:

- **Antibacterial Properties:** Copper has natural antimicrobial properties. Studies have shown that copper can destroy harmful bacteria, viruses, and fungi that may be present in drinking water. Storing water in a copper vessel for a few hours can help purify it and reduce the risk of waterborne diseases.

- **Supports Digestive Health:** Copper is known to stimulate the production of bile, which aids in digestion. Drinking water stored in copper vessels can help balance the digestive system, promote the absorption of nutrients, and alleviate issues like indigestion, bloating, and acidity.
- **Boosts Immunity:** Copper plays a vital role in the proper functioning of the immune system. Drinking water stored in copper vessels regularly can help strengthen immunity and fight off infections, thanks to its antimicrobial and antioxidant properties.
- **Balances the Body's Doshas:** According to Ayurvedic principles, drinking water from copper vessels can help balance the three doshas (Vata, Pitta, and Kapha) in the body. Copper is considered to have a positive impact on all three doshas, promoting overall well-being and balance in the body.
- **Enhances Brain Function:** Copper is a crucial trace element that is involved in several bodily functions, including the proper functioning of the brain. Regular consumption of water stored in copper vessels may improve memory, concentration, and cognitive function, as copper aids in the production of neurotransmitters and the maintenance of brain health.
- **Rich in Antioxidants:** Copper is an essential element for the production of red blood cells and the absorption of iron. It is also rich in antioxidants, which help neutralize harmful free radicals in the body and reduce oxidative stress. This can lead to better skin health and reduced

risk of chronic diseases.

- **Environmental Benefits:** Copper vessels are reusable, making them an environmentally friendly option compared to plastic bottles, which contribute to pollution. By using copper vessels, individuals can reduce their reliance on disposable plastic, contributing to a more sustainable lifestyle.

13. Smearing Cow Dung on Floors

The Practice: In many rural and traditional households, particularly in India, it is common to smear cow dung on the floors, especially during festivals, religious ceremonies, or as a routine cleaning practice. Cow dung is often applied to the floors of kitchens, courtyards, and even temples.

The Truth:

- **Antibacterial and Antifungal Properties:** Cow dung has been used for centuries due to its natural antimicrobial properties. It contains beneficial bacteria and enzymes that can help disinfect the surface and kill harmful germs, bacteria, and fungi. When smeared on the floor, cow dung acts as a natural cleanser, reducing the risk of infections.
- **Pest Repellent:** The application of cow dung is known to help ward off insects and pests, such as mosquitoes, flies, and ants. Its antimicrobial properties discourage the growth of harmful microorganisms, creating a cleaner and healthier environment.
- **Cooling Effect:** Cow dung is an excellent natural insulator. In rural areas with hot climates, smearing cow dung on floors helps to keep the environment cool

by lowering the temperature of the floor and the surrounding air. This makes homes more comfortable during hot weather.

- **Air Purification:** The drying of cow dung releases volatile compounds that are believed to purify the air. These compounds are known to neutralize harmful pollutants and improve indoor air quality. Smearing cow dung on the floor can help remove the unpleasant odors in a natural way, providing a fresher environment.
- **Symbol of Purity:** In Hinduism and many other Indian traditions, the cow is considered sacred and a symbol of purity. Cow dung is seen as a substance that embodies sanctity and is often used in rituals to purify spaces and people. The act of smearing cow dung on the floor is a practice that embodies both physical and spiritual cleanliness.
- **Sustainable and Eco-Friendly:** Cow dung is a natural and eco-friendly alternative to chemical cleaning agents. By using cow dung, individuals can reduce their dependence on synthetic cleaners, which may contain harmful chemicals. Moreover, cow dung is biodegradable and can be used as a natural fertilizer in agricultural practices, contributing to sustainability.
- **Cultural and Tradition Preservation:** Smearing cow dung on floors is a practice passed down through generations. It reflects a deep connection with nature and traditional wisdom. Although it may seem unconventional in modern households, it is part of a sustainable and health-conscious lifestyle that values natural resources.

14. Applying Sandalwood Paste

The Practice: Applying sandalwood paste to the forehead or body, especially during religious rituals, ceremonies, or for personal use, is a common tradition in many Indian households. The paste is typically made by grinding sandalwood on a stone slab with water, and it is often applied during prayers, meditation, or to enhance personal grooming.

The Truth:

- **Cooling Effect:** Sandalwood has natural cooling properties, which is why it is often applied on the forehead. In hot climates, it helps to reduce body heat and provides a refreshing, soothing sensation. It can also be used to cool the skin after prolonged exposure to the sun.
- **Anti-Inflammatory and Antiseptic:** Sandalwood is known for its anti-inflammatory and antiseptic properties. When applied to the skin, it can help soothe irritated skin, reduce swelling, and promote healing. This makes it an effective remedy for minor burns, rashes, or acne.
- **Skin Care Benefits:** Sandalwood paste is often used as a natural remedy for skin care. It helps in improving skin complexion by reducing blemishes and pigmentation. Its natural oils hydrate and moisturize the skin, making it feel soft and smooth.
- **Aromatherapy and Stress Relief:** The scent of sandalwood is calming and is often used in aromatherapy to reduce stress, anxiety, and mental fatigue. Applying sandalwood paste on the forehead or temples during meditation or prayers is believed to help

promote mental clarity, focus, and relaxation.

- **Religious and Spiritual Significance**: In many Hindu rituals, the application of sandalwood paste is a way of purifying the body and mind before engaging in spiritual activities. It is considered a sacred act that invokes positive energy, and the fragrance is believed to attract divine blessings.
- **Detoxification:** Sandalwood contains natural compounds that help detoxify the body by drawing out impurities and toxins when applied to the skin. This cleansing effect is why it has been used in traditional beauty treatments and wellness practices for centuries.
- **Anti-Aging:** The antioxidants present in sandalwood help fight free radicals, which are responsible for aging and skin damage. Regular use of sandalwood paste can help reduce wrinkles, fine lines, and promote a youthful appearance.

Conclusion

The health and hygiene practices followed by our ancestors were rooted in deep understanding and respect for the natural world. While some may seem outdated today, their core principles remain relevant and valuable.

IV
Rituals and Worship

Rituals and worship have always been integral to Indian traditions, providing a structure for expressing devotion and maintaining a spiritual connection. However, beyond their religious significance, these practices often carry profound psychological, social, and even scientific value.

By understanding the deeper meanings behind these rituals, we can appreciate how they promote harmony within individuals and communities while fostering a connection with nature and the universe.

1. Lighting a Lamp (Deepam)

The Practice: Lighting oil lamps (often called "Deepam" or "Diya") during prayers, festivals, or in daily rituals is a widespread practice in Indian households, particularly during religious ceremonies and auspicious events. These lamps are usually made from clay, brass, or copper and are filled with oil (often ghee or sesame oil) with a cotton wick.
The Truth:

- **Symbol of Positivity:** The flame of the lamp is a symbol of knowledge, light, and the dispelling of darkness. In spiritual contexts, it represents the removal of ignorance and the arrival of wisdom. The act of lighting a lamp is seen as a ritual to invite positive energy, prosperity, and spiritual enlightenment into the home.
- **Promoting Focus and Mindfulness:** Watching the steady flame of a lamp is said to encourage concentration and mindfulness. The steady flame can have a calming effect on the mind, helping individuals enter a meditative state. This makes it an ideal practice during prayers or meditation, promoting mental clarity and relaxation.
- **Air Purification:** The burning of ghee or oil releases aromatic compounds that purify the air. The smoke from the lamp has mild antibacterial properties, helping to cleanse the environment by reducing harmful bacteria and pollutants. In traditional homes, the practice of lighting lamps was believed to keep indoor spaces cleaner and fresher.
- **Symbolic of the Inner Light:** In many Indian philosophies, the lamp is a metaphor for the inner light that each individual possesses. Lighting a lamp is a

symbolic act of igniting one's inner wisdom, aligning oneself with the divine, and seeking guidance from higher spiritual forces. It reinforces the connection between the external world and inner peace.

- **Sustainable and Eco-Friendly Lighting:** Traditional oil lamps are an eco-friendly alternative to electric lighting. The use of natural oils like ghee, sesame oil, or mustard oil ensures that the practice is environmentally sustainable. The lamps burn cleanly, without the toxic emissions associated with modern lighting sources, making them an eco-conscious way to light the home.

- **Scientific Significance of Light:** The act of lighting a lamp is not just a spiritual ritual; it also has practical benefits. In ancient times, it provided illumination during nighttime activities, allowing people to continue their work or prayers after sunset. The presence of light has been shown to positively affect mood, well-being, and circadian rhythms, providing psychological benefits even today.

2. Offering Flowers to Deities

The Practice: Offering flowers to deities is a common ritual in Hindu worship and is performed in temples, homes, and during festivals. The flowers, typically fresh and fragrant, are placed on the altar or directly in front of the idol of the deity being worshipped. The act is often accompanied by prayers, chanting, and other religious practices.

The Truth:

- **Symbol of Purity and Devotion:** Flowers are considered a symbol of purity, beauty, and divinity. Offering them is a way to show respect, love, and devotion to the deity. The act is believed to elevate the devotee's intentions, turning a simple act into a powerful spiritual offering.

- **Therapeutic and Mood-Enhancing:** Many flowers, such as jasmine, rose, and lotus, have been used in traditional practices not only for their beauty but also for their soothing properties. The fragrance of flowers has been shown to have a positive effect on mood, reducing stress and creating an atmosphere of calm and peace. This makes the practice not only spiritually beneficial but also mentally rejuvenating.
- **Connection to Nature:** The offering of flowers establishes a deep connection with nature, as flowers are natural products of the earth. By presenting flowers to deities, practitioners acknowledge and honor the life force present in the natural world. This practice aligns with the belief in the interconnectedness of all living beings and the divine.
- **Symbolism of Transience:** Flowers are often used in religious offerings to remind practitioners of the transient nature of life. Just as flowers bloom and wither, life is fleeting, and offering flowers symbolizes the impermanence of material existence. This serves as a reminder to focus on spiritual growth and self-realization rather than worldly attachments.
- **Scientific Benefits of Flower Scent:** The natural aromas released by flowers during offerings have been shown to have physiological benefits. The pleasant fragrance can help lower stress hormones, enhance concentration, and improve mental clarity. Certain flowers, like lavender and jasmine, are also associated with improved sleep quality and relaxation.

3. Ringing the Temple Bell (Ghanta)

The Practice: Ringing the temple bell, or "Ghanta," is a customary ritual in Hindu temples and during religious ceremonies. The bell is rung before, during, or after worship to mark the start or completion of prayers. It is often done while offering prayers or invoking the deity's presence in the temple.

The Truth:

- **Scientific Impact of Sound:** Sound has been shown to have an impact on the human body and mind. The ringing of bells creates a sound frequency that resonates with the body's natural frequencies, promoting a sense of calm and peace. The vibrations from the bell can have a calming effect, reducing stress levels and promoting mental clarity. In traditional practices, these sound frequencies are believed to enhance meditation, help people connect with their spiritual selves, and boost overall well-being.

- **The Role of Resonance in Spirituality:** The ringing of the temple bell also ties into the ancient belief that sound, or "Nada," is a form of vibration that can help in achieving spiritual enlightenment. In Hindu philosophy, sound vibrations are said to have a deep connection with the universe's underlying rhythm and harmony. The bell's ringing is thought to resonate with the cosmic sound, "Om," helping individuals attune their consciousness to the universal truth.

- **Symbolic of Invoking Divine Presence:** The sound of the bell is believed to signal the beginning of a prayer or worship session, and its ringing is considered an invitation to the divine to enter the space and bless the worshippers. The clear, resonant sound of the bell is thought to represent the call to the divine, creating a sacred atmosphere conducive to worship and devotion.

- **Purification of the Mind and Environment:** The ringing of the temple bell has a psychological and environmental impact. The sound is considered to purify the surroundings by dispelling negative energies and creating a vibration that is believed to clear the air and cleanse the space. The sound of the bell can also help clear the mind, making it easier for devotees to focus and enter a state of concentration and devotion during their prayers.

- **Marking Time and Transition:** The ringing of the bell signifies the transition from mundane to sacred time. It marks the moment when the devotee's mind shifts from worldly distractions to spiritual focus. The sound of the bell serves as a reminder to be present in the moment, guiding the devotee through the ritual of worship and into a state of mindfulness.

- **Enhancing Social Cohesion and Unity:** In many traditional communities, the temple bell is also a tool for bringing people together. Its sound is heard by everyone in the vicinity, drawing them to the temple and creating a sense of collective spirituality. It fosters social unity and shared devotion, as everyone in the vicinity is brought into a single moment of religious observance.

4. Applying Tilak or Kumkum

The Practice: Tilak or Kumkum is a sacred mark applied to the forehead, typically between the eyebrows, as part of

Hindu worship and cultural practices. It is often applied during religious ceremonies, festivals, or as a daily ritual. The mark can be made with various substances such as kumkum (a red powder), sandalwood paste, or turmeric, depending on the region and occasion.

The Truth:

- **Scientific Explanation of the Third Eye:** The forehead, where the Tilak is applied, is considered to be the seat of the third eye, associated with the pineal gland. The pineal gland is responsible for regulating sleep and wake cycles, producing the hormone melatonin. Applying a mark to this area is thought to stimulate the pineal gland, promoting mental clarity, better focus, and a deeper state of mindfulness. This ritual is linked to improving concentration, enhancing intuition, and fostering inner peace.

- **Symbol of Blessings and Protection:** The practice of applying a Tilak or Kumkum is believed to invoke blessings from the deity being worshipped. The forehead, especially the area between the eyebrows, is considered a significant energy point (known as the "Ajna Chakra" or third eye) in the body, linked to spiritual insight and wisdom. By applying the Tilak, devotees seek divine protection and spiritual guidance, as well as the removal of obstacles in their lives.

- **Therapeutic and Healing Properties:** In ancient practices, the substances used for Tilak or Kumkum—such as sandalwood paste, turmeric, and kumkum—were chosen for their beneficial properties. Sandalwood, for example, has a cooling effect and is believed to soothe the mind, reduce stress, and improve mental clarity. Turmeric has antiseptic and anti-inflammatory properties, which were thought to cleanse and protect the body and mind from harmful energies. Kumkum, made from a blend of turmeric and other ingredients, is thought to have a purifying effect, especially on the spiritual level.

- **Energy Centers and Chakras:** The area where the Tilak is applied is not only the site of the Ajna Chakra but also has a direct connection to the body's energy systems. According to Ayurvedic and yogic traditions, the forehead is a vital energy center that governs wisdom and intuition. Applying a Tilak here is believed to activate these energy centers, helping to balance the body's energies and promote overall well-being.
- **Significance in Social and Cultural Identity:** The practice of applying Tilak or Kumkum also carries cultural significance, representing one's religious affiliation, respect for tradition, and commitment to spiritual growth. It is a visible symbol of the devotee's connection to the divine and serves as a reminder of their spiritual path. In many communities, wearing a Tilak or Kumkum signifies a sense of belonging and identity, not only within the family but also in a larger social or religious context.
- **Psychological Impact:** The act of applying a Tilak can have a psychological impact, creating a ritualistic and calming effect on the mind. By engaging in this practice, individuals experience a sense of mindfulness and intentionality, which promotes positive mental health. The ritual itself can be meditative, helping to reduce stress and anxiety while fostering a greater sense of purpose and inner peace.
- **Enhancing Devotional Focus:** The application of the Tilak is also a way to mentally prepare oneself for prayer

or meditation. It serves as a physical cue to the mind, signaling that the devotee is entering a sacred space and time for spiritual practice. This helps to focus the mind and heart on the divine, reinforcing the devotional intent and enhancing the effectiveness of the spiritual practices that follow.

5. Offering Prasadam (Holy Food)

The Practice: Offering prasadam refers to the sacred food offerings made to deities during religious ceremonies and prayers, which is then distributed among devotees. Prasadam can be fruits, sweets, or cooked dishes, depending on the tradition and deity being worshipped. After being consecrated, prasadam is believed to carry divine blessings.

The Truth:

- **Symbol of Divine Blessing:** Offering food is a way of showing devotion and gratitude. It symbolizes humility, surrender, and a desire to offer the best to the deity. Consecrated prasadam is believed to carry divine blessings, which can be transferred to those consuming it.

- **Nutritional and Health Benefits:** Prasadam often includes ingredients known for health benefits, such as bananas, coconut, or citrus, rich in vitamins and antioxidants. Sweets like laddoos or halwa, containing ghee, jaggery, and dry fruits, are nourishing and beneficial when consumed in moderation.

- **Energy Transfer and Blessings:** Food offered with devotion carries positive energy, linked to the concept of "prana" in Ayurveda and yoga. Preparing and offering food with mindfulness infuses it with high vibrational energy, promoting well-being, peace, and healing.

- **Digestive Health and Rituals:** Prasadam often includes ingredients known for digestive benefits, such as cumin, cardamom, and ginger, which aid digestion, reduce bloating, and stimulate metabolism. These ingredients have therapeutic properties, ensuring prasadam is both spiritually and physically beneficial.
- **Community and Social Bonding:** Offering prasadam fosters a sense of community, as it is shared among devotees, reinforcing social ties and collective well-being. This communal aspect emphasizes generosity and ensures everyone, regardless of background, has access to divine blessings.
- **Psychological and Emotional Healing:** The ritual of offering prasadam is meditative, promoting emotional balance, reducing stress and anxiety. Consuming prasadam can have a calming effect on the mind, enhancing mental clarity and fostering joy and fulfillment.
- **Sacredness of Food:** Food is viewed as sacred in Hindu culture, not just as sustenance for the body but as spiritual nourishment. Offering food to the divine encourages reverence and gratitude, making the act of eating a mindful, elevated, and sacred experience.

6. Performing Circumambulation (Pradakshina)

The Practice: Pradakshina is the act of walking around a sacred object, such as a deity, temple, or altar, in a clockwise direction. Commonly observed during Hindu prayers or temple visits, devotees typically perform pradakshina by walking around the main sanctum or idol, often three times, symbolizing respect, reverence, and devotion.

The Truth:

- **Symbol of Reverence and Devotion:** Circumambulating a deity or sacred object demonstrates respect and submission. The clockwise movement symbolizes alignment with the natural flow of energy in the universe, representing the devotee's spiritual alignment with the divine.
- **Energy Flow and Spiritual Connection:** The clockwise motion mirrors the motion of the sun, moon, and earth, representing cosmic order. Pradakshina is thought to generate and absorb positive energy, helping the devotee spiritually connect with the divine.
- **Psychological and Meditative Benefits:** The repetitive motion of walking and focusing on the deity helps clear the mind, reduce stress, and promote mindfulness. This physical prayer creates a sense of inner peace and spiritual connection, leading to a meditative state.
- **Physical Health and Circulation:** From a scientific perspective, pradakshina improves circulation, enhances joint flexibility, and promotes overall health. The slow pace of walking also calms the nervous system, fostering relaxation and reducing tension in the body.
- **Symbol of the Cycle of Life:** Pradakshina symbolizes life's cyclical nature—birth, growth, decay, and rebirth. The act reflects the journey toward spiritual liberation (moksha), with the deity representing the eternal truth.
- **Cleansing of Negative Energy:** Circumambulation is believed to cleanse the mind and soul of negative

energies, purging impurities and paving the way for spiritual progress. This spiritual cleansing promotes mental clarity and aligns the devotee with divine intentions.

- **Enhanced Focus and Devotion:** Walking around a deity requires physical and mental focus, enhancing the devotee's spiritual experience. Full engagement in the ritual strengthens the connection to the divine and deepens devotion.
- **Social and Cultural Bonding:** Pradakshina, often performed in groups, fosters a sense of community and shared devotion. It strengthens social bonds, promoting unity and collective worship, which enhances the spiritual and social experience among devotees.

7. Offering Incense (Dhoop/Agarbatti)

The Practice: Offering incense during prayers or rituals is a common practice in Hindu households and temples. Incense sticks or dhoop (solid incense) are lit and offered to deities or to purify the environment. The rising smoke is considered a symbol of devotion and is believed to carry prayers to the divine.

The Truth:

- **Aromatherapy and Mental Clarity:** Incense creates a calming and serene environment. The fragrances released during burning have therapeutic benefits, such as promoting relaxation, mental clarity, and focus. Scents like sandalwood, jasmine, or lavender are used to suit specific needs, such as calming the mind or enhancing concentration.

- **Symbol of Purity and Spiritual Connection:** The rising smoke symbolizes the ascent of the soul to the divine. It is believed that the smoke carries the devotee's prayers, wishes, and thoughts to the heavens, creating a spiritual connection with the divine. The fragrance purifies the surroundings and elevates the atmosphere, making it conducive to worship or meditation.

- **Antibacterial and Air-Purifying Properties:** Incense is often made from natural ingredients like resins, herbs, and oils that have antibacterial properties. The smoke is thought to purify the air, eliminating harmful microbes and odors. This practice, once used in homes and temples to maintain hygiene, also contributed to a healthier environment.

- **Mood Enhancement and Emotional Well-Being:** Incense is used to alter mood and create a positive ambiance. Different scents have specific effects on the mind and body, such as promoting relaxation with lavender and sandalwood or uplifting the spirit with rose and citrus. This enhances the emotional well-being of the devotee, fostering feelings of tranquility and positivity.

- **Regulation of Breathing and Meditation:** The act of lighting incense and inhaling its smoke during meditation helps regulate breathing and calm the body's autonomic nervous system. This aids in slowing the breath and steadying the mind, enhancing the quality of meditation and encouraging focus and tranquility.

- **Historical and Cultural Significance:** Incense has been used for thousands of years in religious contexts across various cultures, including Hinduism. The burning of incense in temples is a way to honor deities, cleanse the environment, and invite the divine presence into sacred spaces.

8. Chanting Mantras

The Practice: Chanting mantras is an integral part of spiritual and religious practices in Hinduism and other traditions. A mantra is a sacred word, phrase, or sound repeated during meditation, prayers, or rituals. The repetition of these words is believed to invoke divine energy and bring positive changes. Mantras can be chanted aloud or silently, often following a rhythmic or repetitive pattern.
The Truth:

- **Vibrational Frequency and Healing:** Mantras are composed of specific sounds and syllables that produce vibrational effects, aligning the body's energy with universal energy. For example, chanting the mantra "Om" connects one with cosmic vibrations, fostering inner peace and healing.
- **Brain Wave Activity and Mental Focus:** Studies suggest that chanting mantras can affect brain wave activity, leading to a calm, focused mind. The rhythmic repetition of mantras induces a meditative state, reducing stress, improving concentration, and promoting mental clarity.
- **Stress Reduction and Emotional Healing:** Chanting mantras triggers the parasympathetic nervous system, lowering heart rate and blood pressure, promoting relaxation, and alleviating anxiety. Research, such as studies from Harvard Medical School, shows that mantra chanting can significantly improve emotional well-being.

- **Activation of the Throat Chakra:** Chanting mantras stimulates the throat chakra (Vishuddha), which governs communication and self-expression. This practice helps enhance clarity in expression and promotes self-healing by releasing emotional blockages.
- **Affirmation and Positive Thought:** Chanting mantras serves as a form of affirmation, helping to reprogram the subconscious mind and cultivate a positive mindset. Mantras like "Om Mani Padme Hum" are believed to invoke compassion, encouraging kindness and goodwill.
- **Scientific Support for Sound Healing:** Sound frequencies used in mantras can influence brain function and mental health. Similar to sound therapy, chanting has therapeutic effects, reducing insomnia, anxiety, and depression, and promoting relaxation and sleep.
- **The Power of Intent and Mindfulness:** The power of chanting mantras lies in the focus and intention behind them. When chanted mindfully with purpose, mantras are believed to manifest positive outcomes, whether for healing, protection, or spiritual growth.
- **Cultural and Spiritual Tradition:** Chanting mantras is deeply embedded in Indian spiritual traditions. Ancient texts like the Vedas, Upanishads, and Puranas describe mantras as sacred sounds that bring one closer to divine consciousness and spiritual liberation (moksha).
- **Spiritual Protection and Positive Energy:** Mantras are believed to create a shield of positive energy, protecting the chanter from negative influences and promoting harmony and prosperity. This is why they are often chanted during auspicious occasions and religious ceremonies to invoke blessings and ward off negativity.

9. Sprinkling Holy Water (Gangajal)

The Practice: In Hindu tradition, Gangajal (water from the holy river Ganges) is considered sacred and is commonly sprinkled in homes, temples, and on people or objects for purification and spiritual blessings. It is used during religious rituals, prayers, and ceremonies as a symbol of divine grace and to invoke positive energy.

The Truth:

- **Antiseptic Properties:** Although the Ganges River is polluted in some areas, water from it is believed to have purifying qualities. Scientific studies suggest that Ganges water has natural antimicrobial properties, containing minerals that can kill bacteria and reduce harmful microorganisms, explaining its purification effects.
- **Symbol of Purification:** Sprinkling Gangajal symbolizes cleansing both physically and spiritually. It is believed to cleanse negative energies, and on a practical level, it represents the washing away of dirt, impurities, and toxic influences, aiding renewal and transformation.
- **Connection to Sacred Water:** The Ganges River is revered as the embodiment of the goddess Ganga, believed to wash away sins and purify the soul. Sprinkling Gangajal helps maintain this sacred connection with the divine, purifying the body, mind, and soul, and honoring ancient traditions.
- **Water's Role in Ancient Healing Practices:** In Ayurveda and traditional medicine, water is vital for health and balance. Gangajal, with its unique mineral composition, is believed to promote physical and spiritual healing,

supporting overall wellness and harmony.

- **Scientific Exploration of Sacred Waters:** Modern research shows that sacred waters like Gangajal contain bioactive compounds beneficial for health. Its mineral content, including calcium, magnesium, and potassium, supports hydration, electrolyte balance, and bodily functions.

- **Energy Flow and Sacred Spaces:** Sprinkling Gangajal is believed to shift the energy of a space, enhancing its vibrational frequency and inviting positive, purer energies. This practice is akin to energy clearing techniques in spiritual traditions, like feng shui, used to restore harmony and encourage positive energy flow.

10. Observing Silence (Mauna Vrata)

The Practice: Mauna Vrata, or observing silence, is a spiritual practice in Hinduism where individuals refrain from speaking for a specific period, often during religious observances, retreats, or as part of personal discipline. It is a form of self-control and mental purification, aimed at enhancing spiritual growth, concentration, and fostering inner peace.

The Truth:

- **Mental Clarity and Focus:** Studies show that constant verbal communication and external stimuli can lead to mental fatigue and reduced cognitive function. By refraining from speech, Mauna Vrata helps clear the mind, promotes focus, mindfulness, and a calm, heightened awareness of one's thoughts.

- **Reduction in Stress**: Silence has been proven to reduce stress levels by relaxing the nervous system and lowering cortisol, the stress hormone. By creating a peaceful mental environment, Mauna Vrata reduces anxiety, enhances emotional stability, and promotes relaxation, similar to the benefits of meditation.
- **Enhanced Self-Reflection**: Silence encourages deep self-reflection. Without verbal distractions, individuals can focus inwardly, contemplating their actions, thoughts, and feelings. This internal dialogue fosters personal transformation and emotional healing, helping individuals connect with their true self.
- **Detoxification of the Mind**: Just as physical fasting detoxifies the body, observing silence detoxifies the mind. It provides space for mental rejuvenation, allowing individuals to release mental clutter and negative emotions, offering a necessary reset in a world filled with constant noise.
- **Enhancing Communication Skills**: Though Mauna Vrata involves refraining from speaking, it paradoxically enhances communication. By becoming more attuned to non-verbal cues like body language and facial expressions, individuals improve listening skills, empathy, and a deeper understanding of others.
- **Mindfulness and Meditation**: Practicing Mauna alongside meditation deepens mindfulness. The silence allows for undistracted focus on the breath, sensations, or thoughts, enhancing the meditative state and reducing mental distractions. Scientific studies support that mindfulness meditation improves cognitive function, emotional regulation, and overall well-being.

Conclusion

Rituals and worship in Indian traditions are not just acts of devotion—they serve as tools for mental clarity, physical well-being, and spiritual growth. They remind us of our connection to the divine and the natural world.

V
Dietary Guidelines

Dietary guidelines in ancient Indian traditions are not just about what we eat but also about how, when, and why we eat. These practices were designed with a deep understanding of the body, mind, and nature. Many of these traditions have been passed down through generations and offer valuable insights into maintaining health, preventing illness, and promoting longevity.

In this chapter, we explore how ancient dietary principles were rooted in both science and spirituality, providing practical wisdom for modern living.

1. Fasting and Detoxification

The Practice: Fasting, a common practice in Hinduism, involves voluntarily abstaining from food (or sometimes water) for a specific period. It is often observed during religious occasions as an act of spiritual purification or detoxification of the body. Fasting can range from complete abstention to partial fasting, where certain foods, like grains or meat, are restricted.

The Truth:

- **Detoxification of the Body:** Scientifically, fasting is a potent method for detoxifying the body. When food intake stops, the body shifts to burning stored fat for energy, a process called ketosis. This helps eliminate toxins accumulated in cells, tissues, and organs, allowing the liver and kidneys to function more efficiently and flush out waste products.
- **Improved Digestion and Gut Health:** Fasting allows the digestive system to rest and reset, which improves its

function. This leads to better digestion and nutrient absorption once food is reintroduced. Fasting can help alleviate bloating, indigestion, and constipation, while also supporting the growth of beneficial gut bacteria, enhancing immunity and overall gut health.

- **Weight Management and Cellular Regeneration:** Fasting is a known weight management strategy, but it also promotes cellular regeneration. During fasting, the body engages in autophagy, breaking down and removing dysfunctional cells, including damaged proteins and cellular waste. This process supports longevity, prevents disease, and helps maintain a healthy body.

- **Reduction of Inflammation:** Chronic inflammation is the root cause of many diseases, including arthritis and heart disease. Fasting has been shown to reduce inflammatory markers by allowing the body to enter a repair state when not processing food. This can improve joint health, cardiovascular function, and decrease the risk of developing inflammatory conditions.

- **Mental Clarity and Cognitive Benefits:** Fasting enhances mental clarity by promoting the production of brain-derived neurotrophic factor (BDNF), a protein that supports brain health and neuron growth. Studies show that fasting can improve concentration, memory, and protect against neurodegenerative diseases like Alzheimer's. It also decreases brain inflammation, contributing to better mental clarity.

- **Spiritual and Emotional Benefits:** In Hinduism, fasting is a method of cleansing not just the body, but also the mind and spirit. It helps increase spiritual awareness by focusing less on material needs and more on the divine. Emotionally, fasting cultivates self-discipline, reduces attachment to desires, and promotes inner peace, fostering greater emotional resilience.

- **Balance of Energy:** Fasting helps balance the body's energy levels. During fasting, the body enters a state of "rest and repair," conserving energy that would otherwise be spent on digestion. This energy is used for bodily repair and rejuvenation, leading to better stamina and vitality.

- **Hormonal Regulation and Insulin Sensitivity:** Fasting plays a key role in regulating hormones, particularly insulin. By restricting food intake, fasting improves insulin sensitivity, helping manage blood sugar levels and reducing the risk of type 2 diabetes. It also helps balance other hormones, including growth hormone, which supports muscle repair, and leptin, which regulates hunger.

- **Scientific Backing of Ancient Practices:** Fasting practices rooted in Hindu traditions have gained scientific validation. Research shows that fasting mimics the effects of calorie restriction, which has been proven to enhance longevity and improve metabolic health. Ancient fasting practices are now recognized for their genuine health benefits, contributing to physical and spiritual well-being.

2. Eating Fresh and Homemade Meals

The Practice: In Indian households, preparing and consuming fresh, homemade meals is a daily tradition. Locally sourced ingredients, fresh vegetables, and herbs are used to emphasize wholesome, freshly cooked food over processed or packaged alternatives.

The Truth:

- **Nutritional Value:** Freshly prepared meals from natural ingredients are nutritionally superior, offering essential vitamins, minerals, and antioxidants that are often lost in processed foods. Cooking at home ensures meals retain their full nutritional value and quality.
- **Healthier Ingredients:** Homemade meals prioritize unrefined oils and natural spices like turmeric and ginger, which provide anti-inflammatory, antibacterial, and digestive benefits. Harmful additives, preservatives, and excess salt or sugar are avoided, promoting better health.
- **Improved Digestion:** Fresh meals, often including fermented foods like idli or curd, support gut health and ease digestion. They lack artificial flavorings or preservatives, making them easier to digest and more balanced in nutrient composition.
- **Better Portion Control:** Cooking at home allows control over portion sizes, preventing overeating common with restaurant meals. Homemade food can be customized to individual dietary needs, ensuring balanced nutrition and healthier weight management.
- **Cultural Connection:** Preparing and eating homemade meals strengthens family bonds, preserves culinary traditions, and fosters mindful eating. This practice encourages individuals to savor meals, enhancing appreciation for food and culture.
- **Traditional Techniques:** Home cooking retains traditional methods using fresh ingredients, preserving nutrition and flavor. Knowledge of specific herbs, spices, and grains, passed through generations, contributes to the health benefits of Indian cuisine.

- **Mental Well-being:** The process of cooking is therapeutic, reducing stress and promoting relaxation. Sitting down to enjoy a home-cooked meal provides emotional satisfaction and counters the fast-food culture of modern life.
- **Environmental Impact:** Homemade meals use fresh, local ingredients, minimizing packaging and reducing food waste. This practice has a smaller carbon footprint, contributing to sustainability and environmental conservation.
- **Reduced Chemicals:** Processed foods contain preservatives and artificial additives harmful to long-term health. Homemade meals avoid these chemicals, offering safer, natural alternatives for better health and longevity.
- **Scientific Backing:** Studies highlight that diets rich in fresh vegetables, fruits, and whole grains reduce risks of chronic diseases. The Indian tradition of eating fresh, homemade meals aligns with scientific recommendations for optimal health.

3. Eating in Moderation (Ahara or Sattvic Diet)

The Practice: In Indian tradition, eating in moderation and following a sattvic diet (one that promotes purity, clarity, and balance) is considered a key component of maintaining good health and spiritual well-being. This practice encourages individuals to consume only what is necessary to nourish the body, mind, and soul, avoiding excess or indulgence in food.

The Truth:

- **Balanced Nutrition:** Moderation in eating ensures a balanced intake of essential nutrients while preventing overloading the body. A sattvic diet of whole foods promotes optimal health, aligning with modern nutritional principles that emphasize balanced macronutrient and micronutrient intake.
- **Weight Management:** Moderation helps prevent overeating, a major cause of weight gain and chronic diseases. Focusing on portion control and mindful eating reduces the risk of obesity, diabetes, and cardiovascular issues, contributing to better long-term health.
- **Digestive Health:** Eating in moderation supports a healthy digestive system by preventing overload. Excessive food intake can lead to toxins and digestive problems, while moderate portions ensure better absorption of nutrients and efficient waste elimination.
- **Sattvic Foods for Mental Clarity:** Sattvic foods, such as fresh fruits, vegetables, and whole grains, are believed to have a calming effect on the mind, improving clarity, focus, and emotional balance. These foods aid spiritual growth and enhance concentration during meditation or prayer.
- **Prevention of Chronic Diseases:** Moderation in food intake helps reduce the risk of heart disease, diabetes, and hypertension. The sattvic approach focuses on natural, unprocessed foods and portion control, aligning with modern medical guidelines for preventing chronic illnesses.
- **Spiritual Well-being:** The sattvic diet not only promotes physical health but also supports spiritual growth. By avoiding overindulgence, individuals maintain balance, enabling a clearer mind for meditation, mindfulness,

and other spiritual practices.

- **Scientific Validation of Moderation:** Research supports the principle of moderation in diet, showing that caloric restriction can extend lifespan and reduce the risk of age-related diseases. This practice aligns with current health recommendations for weight management and longevity.
- **Mental and Emotional Benefits:** Moderation fosters emotional stability by avoiding the extremes of overeating or unhealthy food indulgence. Mindful eating promotes a balanced relationship with food, contributing to emotional well-being and a calm, stable mind.
- **Cultural Relevance:** Eating in moderation is deeply rooted in Indian culture, symbolizing self-discipline and balance. This practice reflects the belief that food should nourish the body and support spiritual growth, not serve as a means of indulgence or excess.

4. The Concept of Satvik, Rajasic, and Tamasic Foods

The Practice: In traditional Indian dietary practices, food is categorized into three types: **Sattvic**, **Rajasic**, and **Tamasic**. These categories are rooted in the ancient philosophy of **Triguna**, which refers to the three fundamental qualities or energies (Gunas) that govern all aspects of life, including food. The type of food we consume is believed to influence not just our physical health, but our mental and spiritual well-being as well.

- **Sattvic Foods** are considered pure, light, and nourishing, promoting clarity, peace, and spiritual growth.
- **Rajasic Foods** are stimulating, intense, and energizing, often associated with passion, activity, and restlessness.
- **Tamasic Foods** are heavy, dull, and inert, believed to promote lethargy, ignorance, and confusion.

The Truth:
Sattvic Foods:

- **Nature**: Sattvic foods are fresh, natural, and organic, usually consumed in their simplest form without excessive processing or cooking. These include fruits, vegetables, whole grains, nuts, seeds, legumes, and dairy products such as milk and ghee.
- **Benefits**: These foods are believed to promote a calm, clear, and focused mind. They are rich in nutrients that support health and vitality while also helping in spiritual practices by keeping the mind sharp and free from distraction. Sattvic food is thought to enhance mental clarity, peace, and emotional stability.
- **Scientific Insight**: Sattvic foods, such as fruits and vegetables, are nutrient-dense and high in antioxidants, vitamins, and minerals that support bodily functions and prevent disease. These foods are also high in fiber, promoting good digestive health and overall vitality. The practice of eating simple, unprocessed foods aligns with modern concepts of a balanced, plant-based diet for optimal health.

Rajasic Foods:

- **Nature**: Rajasic foods are spicy, salty, sour, or bitter in taste and are often stimulating in nature. These foods are designed to provide energy and are typically consumed during times of activity or high energy demand. Examples of Rajasic foods include caffeinated drinks, fried foods, spicy dishes, and highly seasoned or pungent foods.
- **Benefits**: Rajasic foods can increase energy and focus temporarily, but when consumed excessively, they are believed to lead to restlessness, irritability, and emotional instability. These foods are associated with heightened sensory experiences and mental agitation, often leading to overactivity or stress.
- **Scientific Insight**: Modern science supports the idea that highly stimulating foods, such as caffeine, sugar, and spicy dishes, can boost short-term energy and alertness. However, overconsumption can lead to physical and mental imbalances, including stress, anxiety, and digestive disturbances. High-sugar and fatty foods can also contribute to weight gain and chronic health issues, including heart disease and diabetes.

Tamasic Foods:

- **Nature**: Tamasic foods are considered dull, heavy, and processed. These foods are believed to promote lethargy, confusion, and mental fog. Examples include stale, overcooked, or processed foods such as canned items, reheated food, fast food, and alcohol. Tamasic foods often lack vital energy and are associated with ignorance or darkness.

- **Benefits**: Tamasic foods are believed to decrease vitality and promote negative mental states such as depression, confusion, and apathy. These foods are thought to slow down metabolism, leading to sluggishness and poor digestion.
- **Scientific Insight**: There is scientific evidence that consuming excessive amounts of processed foods, fast foods, and alcohol can lead to a range of physical and mental health problems, such as obesity, digestive issues, fatigue, and depression. Tamasic foods are often high in unhealthy fats, sugars, and artificial additives that can disrupt the body's natural balance and contribute to chronic diseases.

5. Drinking Warm Water

The Practice: Drinking warm water, especially in the morning or after meals, is a common practice in many Indian households. It is often recommended for its supposed health benefits, such as aiding digestion and detoxification.

The Truth:

- **Improved Digestion**: Drinking warm water helps stimulate the digestive enzymes, promoting better digestion and reducing bloating. Warm water is known to dissolve food more easily, allowing for smoother digestion and helping to break down the food in the stomach. It is particularly beneficial after meals as it helps in the process of digestion by supporting the body's natural enzymatic activities.

- **Detoxification**: Warm water assists in flushing out toxins from the body. It helps in stimulating the kidneys, thereby supporting the detoxification process. By promoting blood circulation and sweating, it aids in releasing accumulated waste from the body, keeping the skin clear and the body refreshed. The warm temperature also increases the body's internal temperature, which boosts the body's ability to eliminate toxins effectively.

- **Relief from Constipation**: Warm water helps in softening stool and improving bowel movement. It can act as a natural laxative, helping to relieve constipation without relying on chemical-based solutions. Consuming warm water in the morning can stimulate bowel movements and ensure smoother digestion throughout the day.

- **Scientific Insight**: Drinking warm water has been studied for its positive effects on digestion. A study in the *International Journal of Scientific Research* suggested that warm water may support faster digestion compared to cold water, which can constrict blood vessels and slow down the digestive process. Warm water helps increase the rate of gastric juices production and promotes better digestion.

- **Hydration and Circulation**: While cold water can constrict blood vessels, warm water promotes better blood circulation. This not only helps in digestion but also encourages a more efficient delivery of nutrients to cells and organs. Additionally, warm water helps keep the body hydrated more effectively because it is absorbed more rapidly than cold water, which the body may need to warm up first.

6. Spices and Herbs in Cooking

The Practice: Using a variety of spices and herbs in cooking is a hallmark of Indian cuisine. From turmeric and cumin to coriander and cardamom, these ingredients are not only integral to flavor but are also thought to offer a range of health benefits. In many Indian households, the use of these spices is often guided by ancient traditions that emphasize balance and wellness.

The Truth:

- **Medicinal Properties**: Many spices and herbs have medicinal properties that have been recognized for centuries in traditional Indian medicine systems like Ayurveda. For example:

- **Turmeric**: Known for its anti-inflammatory and antioxidant properties, turmeric contains **curcumin**, which is shown to reduce inflammation and improve brain function. It is often used to treat various ailments, from digestive issues to skin problems.
- **Cumin**: Rich in iron, cumin has digestive properties and is known to aid in the absorption of nutrients. It has also been shown to help in reducing bloating and gas.
- **Coriander**: Coriander seeds are not only flavorful but are also beneficial for digestion. They have anti-inflammatory and detoxifying effects, helping to cleanse the body of toxins and support liver function.
- **Ginger**: Widely used for its digestive benefits, ginger can help reduce nausea, improve circulation, and relieve symptoms of indigestion.

- **Cardamom**: Known for its aromatic flavor, cardamom also has digestive and detoxifying benefits. It can aid in freshening the breath and promoting healthy digestion.
- **Balancing the Doshas**: In Ayurveda, spices are used to balance the body's three primary energies or **doshas**—Vata, Pitta, and Kapha. Each dosha governs different aspects of the body and mind, and an imbalance in them can lead to health issues. The careful use of spices is believed to restore harmony to the body by stimulating digestion, enhancing metabolism, and improving immunity.

- **Vata**: Spices like ginger, garlic, and cinnamon help to warm and stimulate Vata, which is associated with dryness and coldness.
- **Pitta**: Cooling spices like coriander and mint balance the fiery Pitta dosha.
- **Kapha**: Spices like black pepper, mustard, and chili help reduce the heavy, damp nature of Kapha.
- **Antioxidants and Anti-inflammatory Effects**: Many spices contain powerful antioxidants that protect the body against oxidative stress and reduce inflammation. Chronic inflammation is linked to various diseases, including heart disease and arthritis. Spices such as turmeric, cloves, and cinnamon are rich in compounds that counteract inflammation and support immune function.
- **Scientific Insight**: Modern science has confirmed the health benefits of many traditional spices. Research in the *Journal of Medicinal Food* shows that turmeric, garlic, and ginger have significant therapeutic potential in treating conditions such as arthritis, digestive disorders, and even some forms of cancer. The active compounds

in these herbs have been studied for their ability to fight oxidative stress and support cellular health.

- **Digestive Benefits**: Spices like fenugreek, ajwain, and mustard seeds are commonly used to support digestion. They stimulate the production of digestive enzymes, helping the body break down food more efficiently. For instance, ajwain is often used to relieve indigestion and bloating, while fennel seeds are known to ease gas and promote better digestion.
- **Culinary and Flavor Benefits**: Beyond their health benefits, spices and herbs are also used to enhance the flavor profile of Indian cuisine. They create complex layers of taste and aroma, adding richness to dishes. This balance of flavors is not only pleasing to the palate but is also thought to be vital for good digestion and nourishment.

7. The Role of Ghee (Clarified Butter)

The Practice: Ghee, or clarified butter, is a staple in Indian kitchens, especially in traditional cooking and rituals. It's commonly used in daily meals, religious offerings, and Ayurvedic treatments. Ghee is considered a pure form of butter, obtained by simmering butter to remove its water content, resulting in a rich, golden substance that is both flavorful and revered in Indian culture.

The Truth:

- **Rich in Healthy Fats**: Ghee is a source of **short-chain fatty acids** (SCFAs), which are easily digested and quickly converted into energy. These fats are known to support brain function, promote fat metabolism, and help with the absorption of fat-soluble vitamins like A, D, E, and K.

- **Butyrate**: Ghee is rich in **butyrate**, a short-chain fatty acid that plays a critical role in maintaining gut health. It has anti-inflammatory properties, supports the immune system, and is essential for the health of the cells lining the intestines. Studies have shown that butyrate helps reduce the risk of digestive disorders, such as irritable bowel syndrome (IBS) and Crohn's disease.

- **High in Omega-3 Fatty Acids**: Ghee made from grass-fed cows is rich in **omega-3 fatty acids**, which are essential for heart health. Omega-3s help reduce inflammation, lower cholesterol levels, and improve brain function.

- **Digestive Health**: According to Ayurveda, ghee is considered beneficial for digestion. It is thought to stimulate the secretion of digestive enzymes, enhancing the breakdown of food in the stomach. Ghee also lubricates the digestive tract, which may help improve digestion and reduce constipation. Its high content of butyrate is known to support a healthy gut microbiome by promoting the growth of beneficial bacteria.

- **Anti-inflammatory and Antioxidant Properties**: Ghee contains a range of **antioxidants**, including vitamin E, which help protect the body from oxidative stress. Its anti-inflammatory properties are beneficial in treating joint pain, arthritis, and skin conditions like eczema. Ghee is also commonly used in Ayurvedic massage and topical treatments for its soothing and healing properties.

- **Sacred and Ritualistic Significance**: In Hinduism, ghee holds a sacred status. It is often used in religious ceremonies and rituals, such as **aarti**, where it symbolizes purity, the removal of darkness (ignorance), and the manifestation of divine light. Offering ghee in lamps is believed to invite positive energies and blessings.

- **Culinary Role**: Ghee enhances the taste and texture of food, giving it a rich flavor and aroma that is central to Indian cuisine. It is used in the preparation of various traditional sweets like **ladoos**, **halwas**, and **kheer**. Ghee has a high **smoke point** (about 485°F or 250°C), making it ideal for deep frying and high-heat cooking without releasing harmful compounds. Its stability at high temperatures ensures that it remains safe and nutritious during cooking.
- **Scientific Backing**: Modern science has supported many of the health claims associated with ghee. Research has demonstrated that ghee, when consumed in moderation, can have positive effects on **cholesterol levels**, **gut health**, and **brain function**. Studies have also highlighted the benefits of ghee in traditional **Ayurvedic medicine**, where it is considered a **balancing food** that nourishes the body and mind.
- **Balanced Consumption**: While ghee is rich in fats, it is important to consume it in moderation. Ayurvedic tradition recommends balancing its intake with other foods to maintain optimal health. When used wisely, ghee can be a highly nutritious addition to the diet, promoting overall wellness and vitality.

Conclusion

Dietary practices in ancient India were not based on trends or fads but were rooted in a deep understanding of how food affects the mind, body, and soul. By following these age-old guidelines, we can promote a balanced life, improve our health, and create a sense of harmony with nature.

VI

Environmental Wisdom

This chapter explores environmental practices from Indian tradition that were once dismissed as superstitions. However, when examined through the lens of modern science, we find that these practices are rooted in a deep understanding of the natural world, promoting ecological balance and sustainable living.

1. Not Cutting Trees (Especially Sacred Ones)

The Practice: In Indian culture, cutting trees, especially sacred ones like the **Peepal**, **Banyan**, and **Neem**, is often considered taboo. Many communities believe that these trees hold spiritual significance and are endowed with divine qualities. Certain trees are worshipped in temples, and there are strict cultural practices that discourage harming or cutting them.

The Truth:

- **Biodiversity Conservation**: Sacred trees like the **Peepal** and **Banyan** are essential to maintaining biodiversity. These trees provide habitat and food for a variety of birds, insects, and other wildlife. The Banyan tree, for example, is a "keystone species" that supports a range of organisms, contributing to ecosystem stability.

- **Carbon Sequestration**: Trees play a vital role in combating climate change by absorbing carbon dioxide from the atmosphere. The act of preserving sacred trees contributes to the larger goal of reducing greenhouse gases and maintaining a balanced climate. These trees, particularly large, old trees, have a higher capacity to store carbon compared to younger or smaller trees.

- **Air Quality Improvement**: Trees naturally filter air by absorbing pollutants and releasing oxygen. The sacred trees in many regions are known to help in purifying the air and maintaining a healthy environment for the local community. By preserving these trees, we are safeguarding the quality of air we breathe.

- **Neem (Azadirachta indica)**: Known for its numerous health benefits, **Neem** is often revered in India for its purifying properties. It has antibacterial, antiviral, and antifungal properties, which have been used in Ayurvedic medicine for centuries. **Neem leaves** are commonly used to treat various skin conditions, and its oil is known for promoting oral health and detoxifying the body.

- **Peepal Tree (Ficus religiosa)**: The **Peepal tree** is known for its air-purifying qualities. Studies have shown that it absorbs carbon dioxide during the night and releases oxygen, making it a vital contributor to improving urban air quality. The Peepal tree is also said to have a cooling effect on the body and mind, contributing to calmness and mental peace.

- **Banyan Tree (Ficus benghalensis)**: The **Banyan tree** is known for its medicinal uses in traditional medicine. Its leaves, bark, and roots are used in Ayurvedic remedies for a variety of conditions such as diabetes, digestive problems, and skin ailments. The tree's high level of oxygen production helps to create a serene environment, contributing to mental well-being.

- **Sacred Connection**: In Hinduism, certain trees are considered embodiments of deities and are revered for their spiritual significance. The **Peepal tree** is associated with Lord Vishnu and is often considered a source of divine energy. The **Banyan tree**, which is symbolic of immortality, represents eternal life due to its extensive root system and long lifespan. In many cultures, these trees are believed to be sacred beings that deserve respect and care.

- **Cultural Beliefs**: Ancient Indian texts and rituals emphasize the importance of trees as part of the broader ecosystem. Protecting sacred trees is a way of honoring nature, ensuring harmony between humans, and preserving the sacred balance of life. Many communities follow traditional beliefs that cutting sacred trees brings bad luck or negative energy, reinforcing their cultural significance in maintaining spiritual health.

- **Ecological Benefits**: Modern science supports the importance of preserving trees for ecological reasons. Sacred trees, with their large canopies and deep-root systems, play a significant role in preventing soil erosion, maintaining groundwater levels, and enhancing the local microclimate.
- **Tree Longevity and Ecosystem Services**: The longevity of trees such as the Peepal and Banyan means they contribute over many generations to environmental stability. Their extensive root systems help reduce flooding by absorbing excess water, and their presence in urban areas can significantly improve urban heat islands by providing shade and cooling the environment.

2. Keeping the Kitchen Clean and Pristine

The Practice: Maintaining cleanliness and order in the kitchen is a long-standing tradition in many households. The kitchen is often considered a sacred space, and keeping it clean is seen as a way to show respect for the food prepared there, as well as the people it nourishes.

The Truth:

- **Preventing Contamination**: A clean kitchen helps prevent the spread of bacteria and other harmful pathogens. By regularly cleaning surfaces, utensils, and storage areas, the chances of cross-contamination are reduced, ensuring that food remains safe to eat. Cleanliness is particularly important when handling raw food, such as meat or vegetables, which can harbor bacteria that cause foodborne illnesses.

- **Maintaining Freshness of Food**: A cluttered, dirty kitchen can lead to improperly stored food or spoiled ingredients. Ensuring that your kitchen is pristine helps maintain the freshness of ingredients, reducing waste and making it easier to prepare healthy meals. Cleanliness also plays a role in the preservation of food, as it keeps pests and mold at bay.
- **Promoting Mental Clarity**: According to psychology, a clean environment has a direct impact on mental health. A tidy and organized kitchen promotes a sense of calm and order, making cooking a more enjoyable and less stressful experience. A clutter-free kitchen can reduce feelings of overwhelm and help individuals focus on the task at hand.
- **Positive Energy (Vastu Shastra)**: In Vastu Shastra, an ancient Indian system of architecture and design, the kitchen is considered a place of nourishment and prosperity. A clean and organized kitchen is believed to attract positive energy (Prana) into the home. Dirt and clutter are thought to block the flow of this energy, leading to disharmony in the household. Keeping the kitchen pristine helps ensure that the home is filled with positivity and abundance.
- **Sacredness of the Kitchen**: In many Indian households, the kitchen is viewed as a sacred space where food is prepared with care and devotion. The act of cooking is often seen as an offering to the divine, and maintaining a clean kitchen is a way of honoring that sacred ritual. The cleanliness of the kitchen is believed to directly affect the purity and quality of the food prepared there, ensuring that it nourishes the body and soul.
- **A Symbol of Self-care**: Keeping the kitchen clean is also symbolic of self-respect and care for one's family. It

reflects an individual's commitment to health, well-being, and the well-being of others in the household. A pristine kitchen reflects the mindfulness and effort put into cooking and providing nourishing meals for the family.

- **Balance and Harmony**: Ayurveda emphasizes balance and harmony in all aspects of life, including the food preparation process. A clean kitchen is thought to contribute to the creation of **sattvic** (pure) meals, which are nourishing not just for the body but also for the mind and spirit. In this context, a dirty or disorganized kitchen could create a **tamasic** (unhealthy) environment, affecting the energy of the food being prepared. Cleanliness in the kitchen promotes a balanced atmosphere that supports the preparation of wholesome, life-sustaining meals.

- **Streamlined Cooking Process**: A clean kitchen is more efficient for meal preparation. With everything in its place, cooking becomes easier and faster, reducing the chances of mistakes or accidents. When the kitchen is clutter-free, it's easier to focus on the task at hand, leading to more efficient and enjoyable cooking sessions. This is especially important in households where cooking is done regularly and involves multiple steps.

3. Worshipping the Cow

The Practice: Worshipping the cow is a sacred tradition in many parts of India, especially in Hindu culture. Cows are revered as symbols of non-violence, abundance, and motherly nurturing. It is common to see cows adorned with garlands and worshiped during special festivals, particularly in rural areas.

The Truth:

- **Sacredness of the Cow**: In Hinduism, the cow is often regarded as a symbol of Ahimsa (non-violence) because of its gentle nature. The cow is an embodiment of compassion and nurturing, as it provides milk, a vital source of nourishment, without causing harm. Reverence for cows encourages compassion and care for all living beings, promoting a lifestyle of peace and respect for life.

- **Symbol of Motherhood**: The cow is also associated with the motherly qualities of nurturing and caring, as it provides sustenance in the form of milk for humans, especially in rural communities. Its gentle nature and unassuming presence have earned it the status of "Gau Mata" (Mother Cow) in Indian culture. By worshipping the cow, people express gratitude for the nurturing role it plays in their lives.

- **Connection to Divinity**: In Hindu mythology, the cow is linked to many gods and goddesses, most notably Lord Krishna, who is often depicted as a cowherd. Lord Krishna's love and care for cows reflect their divine status. The cow's sacredness also extends to its association with **Kamadhenu**, the wish-fulfilling cow, which is believed to possess the ability to grant prosperity and abundance. This divine connection deepens the cultural and spiritual reverence for the cow.

- **Ritualistic Worship**: In many Indian households, worshipping the cow involves offering prayers, feeding the cow, or performing ceremonies on certain occasions. The cow is sometimes adorned with flowers and worshipped during festivals like **Gopashtami** and **Diwali**, which are dedicated to cow reverence. These practices symbolize respect for the cow and its role in providing sustenance, both spiritually and physically.

- **Natural Fertilizer**: The dung of cows, known as **gomaya**, has been traditionally used as an organic fertilizer in agricultural practices. It is rich in nutrients like nitrogen, phosphorus, and potassium, which help improve soil fertility. The use of cow dung is an environmentally friendly alternative to chemical fertilizers, which can harm the ecosystem. Furthermore, cow urine has been used in traditional Ayurvedic medicine for its purported antibacterial and antimicrobial properties.

- **Ayurvedic Medicine**: In Ayurveda, cow products like **cow urine** and **ghee** are believed to possess medicinal properties. Cow urine, known as **gomutra**, has been used in traditional Ayurvedic remedies for its detoxifying and healing properties. It is believed to purify the body and treat a variety of ailments, including digestive issues, skin diseases, and infections.

4. Not Sleeping with Feet Facing East

The Practice: In many Indian households, it is a common belief that one should not sleep with their feet facing the east. This practice is widely followed during rest and sleep, particularly in the traditional settings of Hindu households. The position of the body during sleep is considered significant, and specific alignments are believed to have a profound impact on one's health and spiritual well-being.

The Truth:

- **Magnetic and Geomagnetic Field**: According to ancient Indian traditions, the earth is surrounded by a magnetic field, and different directions are thought to align with different energies. The belief is that when we sleep with our feet facing east, we are aligning our body's energy with the Earth's magnetic field in an unfavorable way, leading to potential discomfort or health issues. In contrast, sleeping with the head facing east or towards other specific directions, such as the north or south, is believed to align more harmoniously with the Earth's magnetic forces.

- **Religious and Cultural Connections**: In Hindu philosophy, the east is considered the direction associated with the rising sun, symbolizing new beginnings, enlightenment, and knowledge. However, the feet, which represent the foundation of one's physical being, should not be pointed toward this direction during sleep, as it is believed to disturb the alignment of vital energies (Prana). It is seen as a practice that ensures the peaceful flow of energy in the body while sleeping.

- **Circulation and Alignment**: Some proponents of this belief suggest that sleeping with the feet facing east can lead to imbalances in the body's internal systems. The head, when facing east, is believed to promote mental clarity and rejuvenation, while having the feet pointed in the same direction is said to disrupt the body's energy alignment, leading to disturbed sleep or even physical discomfort.

- **Traditional Ayurvedic Wisdom**: According to Ayurvedic principles, the quality of sleep is essential for overall health. Ayurveda emphasizes maintaining harmony with the body's natural rhythms, which are believed to be influenced by directions. While there may not be a direct scientific basis for the specific position of one's feet, the general principle behind this practice is rooted in the understanding that our health is closely connected to our environment and the natural forces at play.

- **Modern Scientific Perspective**: While modern science has not fully supported the claim that sleeping with feet facing east is inherently harmful, there is an increasing understanding of how the Earth's magnetic fields, circadian rhythms, and environmental factors impact sleep quality. Magnetic fields, for example, have been studied for their effects on human health, but more research is needed to definitively prove the exact impact of directional sleeping. Nonetheless, some individuals find that paying attention to their sleeping position—based on cultural or spiritual beliefs—can contribute to a more restful and balanced state.

Conclusion

The practices we once viewed as superstitions are in fact deeply rooted in ancient wisdom, offering scientific insights that were ahead of their time. By embracing these traditions with an open mind, we can tap into the vast knowledge of our ancestors, benefiting from practices that promote health, environmental sustainability, and spiritual well-being.

VII
Conclusion

Reinterpreting Ancient Wisdom for the Modern Age

As we journey through the pages of this book, we have explored a wide range of Indian traditions and practices that have been deeply ingrained in the fabric of society for centuries. What often appeared as mere superstitions or rituals at first glance have, in fact, shown themselves to be grounded in practical knowledge, ecological understanding, and scientific reasoning. The challenge of today is not to discard these ancient practices but to reinterpret and adapt them in ways that align with modern advancements and needs.

The Need for a Balanced Approach

The rapid pace of technological and scientific progress in recent years has sometimes led us to view traditional wisdom as outdated, irrelevant, or even illogical. However, as we delve deeper into the roots of these practices, we see that they were not just random beliefs, but rather were born out of the observations and insights of people who closely understood their environment, health, and social dynamics.

Rather than dismissing these practices outright, we must focus on understanding the logic behind them, as it aligns with sustainable living, health, and well-being in the modern context. Today, many of these age-old practices are being rediscovered for their relevance in promoting environmental sustainability, improving personal health, and fostering harmony within communities.

Bridging the Gap Between Tradition and Modernity

In the past, knowledge was passed down orally or through written texts, and many of these practices were often tied to religious rituals or cultural customs. With the advent of science and technology, we have gained a deeper understanding of the mechanisms behind what was once deemed mystical or superstitious.

The key is to bridge the gap between tradition and modernity. We do not need to reject these practices, but instead, we should find ways to integrate them into our contemporary lifestyle. This can mean rethinking the way we approach sustainability, health, and community living—ensuring that we honor and preserve the wisdom passed down through generations while adapting it to meet the demands of the modern world.

Learning from the Past, Shaping the Future

Ancient Indian traditions offer us a wealth of knowledge that, when understood and applied correctly, can contribute to a healthier, more sustainable future. The practices that were once tied to spirituality, such as fasting, tree worship, and offering prayers to nature, are now being recognized for their practical benefits in promoting mental and physical health.

The ancient wisdom that has been passed down over millennia is a valuable resource in addressing some of the most pressing challenges of the modern world—such as environmental degradation, rising health issues, and the need for sustainable living. By reinterpreting these traditions through the lens of science and reason, we can gain new insights into how to live in harmony with nature and foster overall well-being.

A New Perspective on Spirituality and Science

In this modern era, spirituality and science are often seen as two distinct entities. However, the ancient Indian worldview embraced the idea that both spirituality and science are interconnected. The practices and rituals discussed throughout this book show that spirituality wasn't just about religious worship; it was about aligning oneself with the natural world, understanding the forces of nature, and living in a way that was beneficial not just for the individual, but for society as a whole.

By reinterpreting these traditions, we can begin to see how spirituality and science complement one another, offering a holistic approach to life that balances the material with the spiritual. This is the essence of ancient wisdom: it integrates the mind, body, and spirit in a way that promotes overall health, environmental sustainability, and a deeper understanding of the world around us.

Looking Forward: A Harmonious Future

As we move forward, it is crucial to continue embracing the wisdom of the past while remaining open to the possibilities that modern science and technology offer. Rather than dismissing traditional knowledge as irrelevant, we should seek ways to integrate these practices into our daily lives. By doing so, we can create a future where the lessons of ancient wisdom guide us toward a more sustainable, healthy, and harmonious way of living.

In the end, the true value of these ancient practices lies not in their mysticism, but in their practical applications. They are a reminder that we do not always have to look to the future for solutions—sometimes, the answers have been with us all along, embedded in the rich cultural and spiritual heritage of our ancestors.

VIII

References and Resources

In this chapter, we present a collection of scientific studies, historical texts, and other resources that support the findings and interpretations discussed throughout the book. These references provide a deeper understanding of how ancient Indian traditions align with modern science and contribute to our understanding of health, sustainability, and well-being.

1. Scientific Studies

- **Role of Fasting in Health**

  - **"Effects of intermittent fasting on health markers in humans"** – A study published in *JAMA Internal Medicine* explores the health benefits of intermittent fasting, such as improved metabolism, blood sugar levels, and cardiovascular health.

- ○ **"Intermittent Fasting: A Comprehensive Review"** – A study in *Cell Metabolism* examines the various benefits of intermittent fasting, including its potential to reduce oxidative stress and inflammation, similar to the health benefits associated with fasting on days like Ekadashi.

- **The Environmental Benefits of Trees**

  - ○ **"Global Forest Resources Assessment"** by the Food and Agriculture Organization (FAO) of the United Nations discusses the role of forests in maintaining ecological balance and combating climate change.
  - ○ **"Tree Canopy and Urban Heat Island Effect"** – A study in *Environmental Research Letters* examines how urban tree canopy coverage can mitigate the urban heat island effect, supporting the ecological wisdom behind tree worship practices.

- **Turmeric and Health Benefits**

  - ○ **"Curcumin: A Review of Its' Effects on Human Health"** – A study published in *Molecules* investigates the various health benefits of curcumin, including its anti-inflammatory, antioxidant, and antimicrobial properties, which support the widespread use of turmeric in Indian traditions.

- **Benefits of Cow Dung as Fertilizer**

  - ○ **"Potential of Cow Dung as a Fertilizer"** – A study in the *International Journal of Environmental Research* *and Public Health* explores the use of cow dung as a natural fertilizer and its environmental benefits, supporting the tradition of revering cows in Indian culture.

2. Historical Texts and Ancient Scriptures

· The Vedas and Upanishads

- The *Rigveda*, *Yajurveda*, and *Atharvaveda* are ancient texts that lay the foundation for many of the spiritual and health-related practices discussed in this book. These scriptures contain hymns, rituals, and philosophical discussions that provide insight into the cultural and scientific aspects of ancient Indian traditions.
- The *Upanishads* further explore the connection between the human body, mind, and the cosmos, offering valuable teachings that align with many of the practices we have discussed, such as fasting, meditation, and connecting with nature.

· Ayurvedic Texts

- Ancient texts such as the *Charaka Samhita* and *Sushruta Samhita* provide detailed guidelines on maintaining health through diet, hygiene, and natural remedies. Ayurveda, India's traditional system of medicine, has long advocated practices like fasting, herbal treatments, and the use of specific foods and rituals to maintain health.

- **The Manusmriti**

  - The *Manusmriti*, an ancient Indian text, addresses topics related to societal conduct, health, and environmental practices. While its views on some aspects are considered outdated in contemporary contexts, it includes guidelines for maintaining a balanced life and respecting the natural world, offering insight into the cultural foundation of practices like tree worship and environmental conservation.

3. Modern Books and Articles

- **"The Science of Spirituality" by Lee Bladon**

  - It integrates science, psychology, philosophy, spirituality, and religion to explore concepts like consciousness, reincarnation, meditation, and the multi-dimensional nature of reality.

- **"India's Sacred Geography" by Diana L. Eck**

  - This book provides a comprehensive understanding of the sacred sites in India and the significance of practices like pilgrimages, tree worship, and offerings to nature, offering insight into the spiritual and ecological wisdom embedded in Indian traditions.

- **"The Ayurveda Bible: The Definitive Guide to Ayurvedic Healing" by Anne McIntyre**

  - This book offers a modern interpretation of the ancient Ayurvedic principles and how they apply to contemporary life, supporting many of the health and lifestyle practices mentioned in the book.

4. Online Resources

- **National Institutes of Health (NIH) - www.nih.gov**

  - The *NIH* website provides a range of scientific studies and research articles on the health benefits of practices like fasting, meditation, and herbal remedies, many of which are discussed in this book.
  - For example, the NIH's section on *"Herbal Medicine" and *"Fasting and Health"* offers a wealth of information supporting the physiological benefits of practices rooted in Indian tradition.

- **International Journal of Environmental Research and Public Health - www.mdpi.com/journal/ijerph**

  - This journal provides studies on the ecological benefits of practices like tree conservation and sustainable farming, which correlate with the environmental practices mentioned in the book.

5. Cultural and Religious Resources

- **The Bhagavad Gita**

  - One of the most revered spiritual texts in India, *The Bhagavad Gita* offers profound insights into the connection between the physical body, the mind, and the universe. Its teachings on self-discipline, mental clarity, and spiritual practices provide a framework for understanding many of the rituals and practices discussed in this book.

- **The Ramayana and Mahabharata**

  - The epics of *Ramayana* and *Mahabharata* not only provide historical narratives but also impart moral and ethical guidelines that have shaped the cultural and spiritual practices in India, including rituals, diet, and environmental respect.

Conclusion

The references and resources provided in this chapter offer a comprehensive understanding of how ancient Indian practices are not only steeped in cultural and spiritual significance but also rooted in science and nature. These studies, texts, and resources help us connect the dots between the past and the present, reaffirming that ancient wisdom is, indeed, relevant and valuable in our modern world.

www.ingramcontent.com/pod-product-compliance
Lightning Source LLC
Chambersburg PA
CBHW040122150726
48005CB00015B/2322